BORN AGAIN TO WIN

Living Life Empowered by the Holy Spirit

Michael R. McComb

DEDICATION

To those who are determined to lay hold of the will of God for your lives. May you experience the life-changing truth that you have been born again to win!

CONTENTS

ACKNOWLEDGMENTS

First I want to say, "I thank Christ Jesus our Lord who has enabled me, because He counted me faithful, putting me into the ministry". (1 Tim. 1.12).

There have been many people in my life who have helped me and made a deposit in my life and ministry, but there are a few who deserve my greatest gratitude.

I want to thank my dear wife, Stephanie, for her encouragement, strength and help to accomplish this work. She has lovingly "prodded" me along - believing I should and could accomplish this. Thank you for the many hours of typing, editing, formatting, and proofreading you have given to make this book a reality. Without you it would not have happened. I love you dearly!

My sincere gratitude goes to my pastor and father in the Lord, Dr. John Hollar, Director of Christ For The Nations Institute. No one has helped me along in ministry more than he. Thank you sir for believing in me – pouring into me through your teaching, counsel and care. I will forever owe you a debt of gratitude. You have been a tremendous example. I once told you, many years ago, "I've got my eye on you!". I'm still watching and trying to grow up just like you!

Brandon Hollar, pastor of Life Unlimited Church, thank you for being my friend – for trusting me and believing in me. I appreciate you so much!

There are two more great men of God who have influenced me tremendously through their teaching ministries. Although we are not close friends, I have spent many, many hours feeding on their teachings that have shaped my doctrine and belief system greatly. Thank you, Andrew Wommack and Pastor Bob Yandian. My life and ministry is marked by your remarkable revelation and anointed ministry gifts.

i

Michael R. McComb

PREFACE

It is my belief that the message of the Kingdom of God, the Word of faith, and the gospel of the grace of God should be married -- united together as one complete message. They should not be exclusive of each other but, rather should be understood to work together to bring a clear understanding of God's intent toward mankind.

As you read this book, you will find that I have endeavored to present these truths in that way. These subjects are vast and this work does not explore them in detail, but I have attempted to make a presentation that will enlighten the reader to grasp a revelation that will free and empower them to win in life.

It is my hope that this book will enhance your understanding and help you to appreciate our good God as you read. It is my prayer that God would open your understanding to comprehend the unsearchable riches of Christ.

Born again to win,

Mike

1 INTRODUCTION

Most people have heard the phrase "born to lose". These words appear in song lyrics, movies and even prominently displayed in biker tattoos. I want to propose to those who believe they were born to lose that we are born again to win! Power for victorious living has been made available for the born again Christian who is filled with the Holy Spirit and who operates in faith.

In this book, I will demonstrate from Scripture that God desires for people to win in life. That's why the Bible speaks of His people with such terminology as is used in Romans 5:17, "For if by the one man's offense death reigned through the one, much more those who receive abundance of grace and of the gift of righteousness will reign in life through the One, Jesus Christ." Because we have received abundance of grace and the gift of righteousness, we can expect to reign in life through Christ -- "We are more than conquerors through Him." (New King James Version, Rom. 8.37).

Faith isn't something we use to obtain victory, rather we should understand that victory has already been won. Therefore, we're not headed toward a victory, we're coming from the victory Jesus won for us at the cross. With this understanding we realize our responsibility is to enforce the victory through faith and authority. This must always be our mindset in life. We are not the sick trying to get healed, we have already been healed by the stripes of Jesus (1 Pet. 2.24). We're not the defeated to trying to win through spiritual warfare; the victory has already been won!

The average Christian believes God can do anything, but the average Christian also believes He has done nothing. It is important to know what God has already accomplished for us through Jesus. Once we understand what was purchased and provided for us it is then a matter of believing and receiving. The understanding that we do not have to move God to act for us will transform us from beggars to receivers. Everything we need has already been provided. Ignorance of what God has done for us through His redemptive plan will hold us in bondage and defeat. Hosea 4:6 says, "My people are destroyed for lack of knowledge…" The world says, "What you don't know won't hurt you." I say, "What you don't know is killing you!" John 8:32 tells us, "And you shall know the truth, and the truth shall make you free". Truth doesn't have the ability to make anyone free. It's only the truth we know that can make us free. If truth had the power to free us, everyone with a Bible would be free.

In this book I will be dealing with Kingdom theology. I believe the average Christian, especially Americans, do not have a kingdom mentality. God's kingdom is unlike any earthly kingdom one has ever known. The most distinguishing element which sets it apart is the fact that every Christian is personally related to the King. This makes the King personally responsible for providing for His people. It is a disgrace to any king when his people aren't provided for.

Dr. Myles Munroe stated it so well:

Our Kingdom is one of abundant supply. We need to

exchange our poverty mindset for a provision mindset. As long as we tend to our Father's business, He will provide everything we need. No matter what our situation, we can focus on the Kingdom, claim our Kingdom rights and say with confidence, "My God will supply." (Rediscovering the Kingdom 157).

Because of the abundant provision and God's unfailing promise and faithfulness every Christian has a responsibility to make it their unceasing goal to maintain their victory in every area of life.

It seems to me many churches who were once strong in proclaiming the power of the baptism of the Holy Spirit no longer preach it as they once did. Many churches and believers have adopted the "seeker friendly" approach due to fear of the manifestation of the Spirit, turning off seekers. This is not the message of the Bible. We need the mighty demonstration of the Spirit in our preaching of the gospel. The great Apostle Paul said in 1 Corinthians 2:4-5, "And my speech and my preaching were not with persuasive words of human wisdom, but in demonstration of the Spirit and of power, that your faith should not be in the wisdom of men but in the power of God." The great mistake of the Church today is that she has attempted to preach the gospel in word only; "For the Kingdom of God is not in word, but in power.(1 Cor. 4.20).

In the book of Acts, the gospel was preached in power. Mark 16:20 tells us, "And they went out and preached everywhere, the Lord working with them and confirming the Word through the accompanying signs. Amen." The early church just took Jesus at His word and went out doing it. They turned their world upside down with the gospel of the Kingdom without all the advantages we have today. With these truths operating in our lives, applied along with a living, vibrant faith, we have definitely been born again to win!

In chapter two, I will discuss a basic understanding of the Kingdom of God with the necessity, as preached by Jesus, that one must be born into the Kingdom. Included in our salvation is standing with God -- complete forgiveness and justification which enables us to benefit from our relationship with the King.

In chapter three, I will explain the need for the "violent to take it by force" (Matt. 11.12). We are to take hold of the will of God with a tenacity that will not be denied and establish the will of God in our lives. This will confront the misunderstanding of the sovereignty of God in our lives. It is true that God is sovereign, but there are many misapplications of His sovereignty. The idea that "God is in control" is a faith killer. Those who believe there is nothing for us to do, remain victims of their circumstances. We must realize we have position with God and standing with Him. In order to rise above our circumstances in life, we must take advantage of our position by exercising faith and authority given to us by our God. God is not working in our lives independent of us. God works in us, through us. We have a part to play in that we must cooperate with Him by faith.

In chapter four, I will explain that the mighty baptism with the Holy Spirit is an enduing of Kingdom power in our lives. I will show how that receiving the Holy Spirit baptism transformed Peter's life from a fearful fisherman to a powerful preacher. This was demonstrated by the fact that he stood up on the Day of Pentecost in Acts chapter two and preached his first sermon resulting in three thousand souls being saved and baptized. I will then explore the next four major examples in the book of Acts where people received the baptism with the Holy Spirit. This will be an exposition of portions of chapters eight, nine, ten and nineteen explaining receiving and ministering the empowering presence of the Holy Spirit. I will demonstrate from Scripture that this is an experience which comes subsequent to salvation.

In chapter five, I will explain some of the purpose and benefits of speaking in other tongues and will show that speaking with other tongues is the initial evidence of the baptism with the Holy Spirit and is available to all. This is not to be a one-time experience, but should become a regular part of our prayer lives, enabling us to communicate mysteries with God (1 Cor. 14.2). When we practice this regularly, we edify ourselves (1 Cor. 14.4), we engage in perfect praise (1 Cor. 14.17) and we pray the perfect will of God (Rom. 8.26-27). I'm convinced the average Spirit-filled Christian does not fully comprehend the value of this gift given to us by God. If we did, we would employ it to a much greater degree in our prayer lives. This explanation will inspire the reader to exercise the gift in prayer, praise and worship in their devotional time with our Father.

In chapter six I will discuss the role of God's ambassadors on earth. As born-again believers we are ambassadors for Christ, tasked with the responsibility of representing Him and His kingdom in the earth. We don't ask for it or have to work to achieve the position; it is bestowed upon us when we accept Jesus as our Savior. As His representatives we've been given the privilege of advancing the Kingdom of God by communicating the message of and goodness of our King. It is vital that we understand the distinctive of the position and the provision God has made for us, enabling us to have success and be effective for Him. I will discuss some characteristics contained within our unique message that all ambassadors share and promote. It is necessary that each individual ambassador catch the vision for his or her life which will propel them forward toward the accomplishment of their destiny.

Catching His Vision for Your Life

We have been created with the capacity for greatness with the potential to do great service and bring pleasure to our God. Revelation chapter four describes the worship scenario taking place as twenty-four elders worship at the throne of God continuously. We're given some of the content of their expression of worship which actually tells us God's purpose in creation: "Thou art worthy, O Lord, to receive glory and honour and power: for Thou hast created all things, and for Thy pleasure they are and were created." (Rev. 4:11 KJV). Our God is not most interested in us for what we can do for Him. He is interested in close, personal relationship with His people and as we relate to Him and worship Him we give Him great pleasure. God is love and has a great desire to have His own special people, thus the reason for commissioning ambassadors to go forth in His name to spread the good news.

Every man and woman was created with the capacity for vision from God for his or her life. We are containers, or holders, of vision. Therefore, everyone has vision. The question is, is the vision they hold for their life from God or from the world? There are two sources from which a person can form vision for their future. The primary source of vision for the ambassador of Christ is God. Vision which is given to an individual by God is one that is special, unique and very important. If a person is not in tune with the Spirit of God in order to understand God's purpose for their life, they can simply be under the influence of a natural, worldly vison. It's often nothing more than survival vision that is self-centered, focused upon its own needs and desires. A person with this type of vision for their life doesn't really know why they exist. They are unaware of God's special purpose and plan for their life. Often Christians equate fulfilling the will of God to being saved, obeying the Bible, and living a good life. Those are commendable things; I don't mean to diminish them, but there is more to Christian life and fulfilling God's will. People become misguided and unfulfilled because they don't know God's specific purpose for their lives. God doesn't want us unfulfilled! Once a person understands God's vision and purpose for them, they then know why they exist. They will then experience direction which will produce a sense of fulfillment and spiritual accomplishment.

I want to give a Scriptural example of changed lives as a result of hearing from our Lord. It is found in Matthew 4:18-22:

> And Jesus, walking by the Sea of Galilee, saw two brothers, Simon called Peter, and Andrew his brother, casting a net into the sea; for they were fishermen. Then He said to them, "Follow Me, and I will make you fishers of men." They immediately left their nets and followed Him. Going on from there, He saw two other brothers, James the son of Zebedee, and John his brother, in the boat with Zebedee their father, mending their nets. He called them, and immediately they left the boat and their father, and followed Him.

Let's understand the scenario. This is early in Jesus' Galilean ministry. He is in Capernaum, walking along the northwestern shore of the Sea of Galilee when He sees Peter and Andrew working their fishing business. Think about what He saw that day. He saw two ordinary men doing ordinary tasks. It wasn't unusual to see fishermen mending their nets on the shore of the Sea of Galilee. He saw two men who loved God and were probably faithful to attend Synagogue worship each Sabbath. But, these were men who had no vision for their lives except for the one they got from the world which was to get up each day, work their fishing business, and sell the catch to earn a living and provide for their family. Please don't misunderstand me; there's nothing wrong with a good work ethic or being a responsible employee and provider for our family. I simply want to make the point that there is more to fulfilling the will of God.

On that day, Jesus walked up to these good men and said, "Follow Me and I will make you fishers of men." Now think about what it sounded like to them. It must have impacted them in such a way that they thought, "That's something greater than we've ever heard about ourselves!" No one had spoken that way to them before. Peter probably wasn't voted most likely to succeed in His graduating class. The Son of God said something to them that day which changed them forever. It impacted them in such a way that "They immediately left their nets and followed Him." Jesus planted a seed of vision in their hearts and then they knew why they were created! They existed for more than working their fishing business.

If we will allow Him, Jesus will do the same for us. This doesn't necessarily mean every believer has to leave their business or vocation to fulfill their call. There are many things God could call us to do other than preaching in a pulpit. We need strong, capable believers invading every area of our culture; ambassadors for Christ impacting our world! As God plants the seed of vision, know it is special, unique, and very important to Him that it is fulfilled.

2 BORN INTO THE KINGDOM OF GOD

If a preacher were to ask a group of average Christians, "Why did Jesus come to the earth?" no doubt there would be many different responses given. There is a scriptural one-verse answer – "For this purpose was the Son of God manifested, that He might destroy the works of the devil." (1 Jn. 3.8). You could paraphrase it like this; Jesus came to undo all the devil has done. Unfortunately, we are living in a fallen world. God isn't the author of the evil and confusion that exists in the world today. In the Garden of Eden when Adam and Eve sinned, mankind was transferred from the hand of God to the hand of Satan. Satan became man's new owner and at that time became the god of this age (2 Cor. 4.4).

Man's bondage to Satan eventually became so complete that Paul the Apostle stated in Romans 7:14, "For we know that the law is spiritual, but I am carnal, sold under sin." Under Satan's control the separation between God and man became so great that the Bible says we were "alienated and enemies in our minds through wicked works" (Col. 1.21). Jesus came to release us from bondage and reconcile us to God. This is called redemption. His death was our substitutionary sacrifice. He paid our penalty so we could have life, forgiveness, and freedom!

Built into God's program before the creation was an arrangement for the redemption of the fallen human race. That is the death of Jesus Christ for the sins of the world was neither plan B for, nor a patchwork on, a creation gone awry. He is 'the Lamb of God that was slain from the creation of the world' (Romans 13:8). Provision was decreed by the wisdom of God's foreknowledge, even before the fall in the Garden (see Eph. 1:4). Christianity is not a latecomer among the religions of the world; it was instituted in the mind of God before the dawn of time. (Menzies and Horton 97).

From God's perspective, the plan of redemption was formulated in the mind of God from before the foundation of the world. Ephesians 2:1 says, "And you He made alive, who were dead in trespasses and sins." When God looked down through the corridor of time, Ephesians 2:1 tells us what He saw. He saw us dead in trespasses and sins.

From our perspective, redemption is freedom, release and reconciliation to God! Because of the redemptive work of Christ on Calvary's cross and our faith in the free gift of God's grace, we now have relationship with our God and have the distinct privilege of knowing Him as our Father! The Apostle Paul continues in chapter two of Ephesians to explain the goodness of God extended to us, even while dead in trespasses and sins.

But God, who is rich in mercy, because of His great love with which He loved us, even when we were dead in trespasses, made us alive together with Christ (by grace you have been saved), and raised us up together, and made us sit together in the heavenly places in Christ Jesus, that in the ages to come He might show the exceeding riches of His grace in His kindness toward us in Christ Jesus. For by grace you have been saved through faith, and that not of yourselves; it is the gift of

God, not of works, lest anyone should boast. (Eph. 2.4-9).

This great plan of redemption is based on God's abounding grace. When we were dead in our sins, deserving of punishment, God was rich in mercy. Mercy is that part of God's grace which holds back what we deserve! In addition, in the exceeding riches of His grace, His kindness was extended to us! Kindness is that part of God's grace which gives us what we do not deserve! The free gift of salvation has been made available by His grace and is now received by faith.

It is by Christ Jesus that God has provided a complete, perfect salvation. The reason God must provide such a salvation is that every mouth must be stopped and all the world become guilty before God. If there is any lack, if there is any area of life in which God has not accepted responsibility and made provision, then man or Satan can accuse God of being unjust. However, if God has assumed the responsibility for the needs of man, then man cannot gainsay God. As I meditate upon this great salvation, I am convinced that God has made a complete provision, and the only reason for failure or lack is that we do not avail ourselves of the grace of God. In each situation in life I recognize that Jesus has provided a fullness. (Voight 4).

It truly matters what we believe about God. If a person doesn't believe Jesus is Savior of the world, that doesn't change who He is. It doesn't change the fact that millions of people around the world are being saved; it just means that person won't experience Jesus as their Savior. If a person doesn't believe God heals, it doesn't change who God is or that multitudes regularly receive healing. It just means that person won't know God as their healer. If a person believes God is weak and powerless, it doesn't mean that God is weak or powerless. It just means that person will have a weak and powerless God. God can only be to us what we believe Him to be. God is not moving in our lives independent of us. No, God works in us, through us. It matters what we believe. We have to cooperate with Him by faith in order to receive His best. The same can be said about God's goodness. Many people don't believe God is good. But that doesn't change who God is. God is good even if no one believes it. Often people accuse God of being responsible for tragedy or crisis or bad things that happen. The simple theological belief that God is good and the devil is bad would prevent a lot of bad doctrine. Goodness is not simply another one of God's attributes. Goodness is not just something God does. No! Good is what God is. God is not good because of what He does. No, God does good because He is good. This is what the Scripture teaches us: "Oh, taste and see that the Lord is good;" (Ps. 34.8) as well as "Oh, give thanks to the Lord, for He is good!" (Ps. 107.1). Good is what God is, and He cannot be changed. Bear with me in a little folly to illustrate this.

I conduct a weekly Sunday evening Chapel service at the Kyle Correctional Center in Kyle, Texas. Each week I use a small portable, tabletop lectern which is made of plywood to preach from. Let's pretend one week I decide to take the week off, and fly to Las Vegas for a well-deserved week of rest and relaxation -- a week of partying, gambling, drinking, and womanizing! I spend the week in undisciplined, prodigal living and return home where I faithfully conduct my chapel service on the following Sunday. I walk in and take my place behind my plywood lectern. Amazingly, the lectern is still plywood! My week's performance didn't change it at all! Now, let's say I decide to spend the following week seeking God. I decide to take a week, fly to Colorado for six days of praying, fasting, and seeking God through His Word in the beautiful, serene mountains. I fly home at the end of the week, with a slight sunburn from exposure to the glory of

God! After a great week of godly and disciplined living I return to my Chapel service, take my place behind my plywood lectern and amazingly it is still plywood! My performance didn't change it at all! Why? Because plywood is what it is. It is plywood and nothing I do can change that. God is good and there is nothing we can do to change that fact. When I perform well, God is good! When I perform poorly God is good. God is what He is regardless of what we do!

Likewise, the Bible teaches us God is love, "God is love, and he who abides in love abides in God, and God in him." (1 Jn. 4.16). Love is what God is. His love for us is totally based upon His nature and character, not ours. This means God loves us and there's nothing we can do about it. When we are good God loves us; when we are bad God loves us! God's love for us is not based on our performance, it is based upon Him…His nature and character. Love is what He is! This understanding of God's unconditional love and goodness will benefit us tremendously in relating to, and receiving from Him. Because God is working in us, through us as we cooperate with Him by faith, His kind disposition extends that love and goodness to us at all times!

Jesus said, "I am the way, the truth, and the life. No one comes to the Father except through Me." (Jn. 14.6). He is not just one of many ways to the Father. He is the only way! Jesus is not an alternate truth; He is the life. Someone might say, "Preacher you sure are dogmatic!" Well, excuse me, but I am just as dogmatic as Jesus was about this! Jesus is our salvation: "He who has the Son has life; he who does not have the Son of God does not have life." (1 Jn. 5.12). It is His life in us which makes us whole. All that Jesus is to us and has provided for us is summed up by the Apostle Paul in Colossians 2:9-10, "For in Him dwells all the fullness of the Godhead bodily; and you are complete in Him, who is the head of all principality and power."

The Mission of the King and His Kingdom

Understanding the Kingdom is foundational to all we learn and teach in Christianity. From the beginning of Jesus' ministry, the message of the Kingdom was His focus. But even prior to His ministry, God had raised up John the Baptist to prepare the way for the King and His kingdom. John the Baptist's ministry was not coincidental to the birth of Jesus. He was a necessary part of what God did to prepare the world to receive the Messiah/King and His kingdom message. For a period of more than four hundred years after the last Old Testament prophet Malachi's ministry, God was silent.

> No canonical records exist for the four-hundred-year period between the return from Babylon and the birth of Jesus, but an understanding of the historical and religious developments during this time is critical to our understanding of the New Testament world. Jesus' ministry and the development of the early church take place within this new context and are shaped, at least in part, by more recent events as well as by Israel's Exodus, kingdom, and the Exile. If the book of Malachi was completed in about 450 B.C., then the period under consideration begins at that point and continues until the angel's announcement of the birth of John the Baptist (Lk. 1.11-17) (Hayford, "Bible Handbook" 507).

At the end of that four-hundred-year period of silence, God raised up John the Baptist to announce and prepare the way for the coming of His Son. Matthew 3:1-3 speaks to us about John the Baptist's ministry and message:

> In those days John the Baptist came preaching in the wilderness of Judea, and saying, "Repent, for the kingdom of heaven is at hand!" For this is He who was spoken of by the prophet Isaiah, saying: "The voice of

one crying in the wilderness: 'Prepare the way of the LORD; Make His paths straight.'"

Isaiah prophesied about His ministry. He was sent as a forerunner, to prepare the way of the King and as an announcer of the coming kingdom! Although we read about him and his ministry in the New Testament, John the Baptist was an Old Testament prophet. Of course, Jesus had not yet been to the cross. John was the most unique prophet in all the Bible. All previous prophets could only speak of the coming of the Messiah/King, but John had the distinct privilege of announcing, presenting, and baptizing the King!

Now notice his message was not about religion; it was about the Kingdom of heaven. "Repent for the Kingdom of heaven is at hand" (v. 2). The first call of the Kingdom was repentance. The word "repent" comes from the Greek word *metanoeo* which is defined by Strong's Concordance as, "to think differently or afterwards, i.e.: reconsider". (Strong's #3340).

So we can see then, repentance is a change of mind which results in a change of direction. True Bible repentance does not mean weeping, crying or sorrow. True repentance will bring a godly sorrow, and it may affect your emotions, but if you didn't turn and go the other way, you didn't repent! John the Baptist was dealing with a Jewish mindset and the first thing he did was exhort them to change the way they thought about the Kingdom. The Jews were looking for their Messiah/King, but He didn't come the way they thought. He didn't live in a palace. He wasn't a conquering general there to deliver them from the Romans. John announced the "Kingdom of Heaven is at hand." (v.2). This means the Kingdom is here, not two decades, or two centuries or a millennium away. The Kingdom is near because the King is here!

Jesus' Kingdom Message

Jesus' message from Matthew chapter four begins with Jesus being led by the Spirit into the wilderness to be tempted by the devil and when the temptations were ended, Luke's account records, *"Jesus returned in the power of the Spirit"* (Lk. 4.14). I have much to say about the empowering presence of the Holy Spirit that I will deal with in chapter four, but for now I will simply point out if Jesus needed the power of the Spirit, how much more do we need the Holy Spirit's power operating through us?! After John the Baptist's short but radical ministry he was placed in prison and Jesus began His Galilean ministry in Capernaum. Matthew 4:17 says, "From that time Jesus began to preach and say, 'Repent, for the Kingdom of Heaven is at hand'"; the same message John preached, to change the way they think about the Kingdom. It suggests the inauguration of the King had begun!

The Jewish mindset was that the Kingdom was a far off time and place. Often, Christians think the same way and need the same message today. When the average Christian thinks of the Kingdom of Heaven they think of a far off time or a far off place. Content and complacent, often compromising, they're just waiting for the Kingdom to come; waiting for the rapture of the church to rescue them from a world on the brink of overcoming them! This is not supposed to be the Church's mindset! Jesus said the Kingdom is at hand. We're not supposed to wait for it; we are to advance it. We are to lay hold of the will of God and establish the Kingdom in our lives and on the earth!

This is exactly what Jesus taught in the Lord's Prayer, which would be more appropriately called the model prayer, "In this manner, therefore, pray: Our Father in heaven, hallowed be Your name. Your kingdom come. Your will be done on earth as it is in heaven." (Matt. 6.9-10). Jesus taught us to pray the will of God would be done on the earth just as it is being done in heaven! We have a part to play in establishing the will of God in the earth. God's desire is to influence earth from heaven through kingdom representatives! This will be addressed in greater detail in chapter six.

John the Baptist's and Jesus' assignment was to introduce a knowledge of the Kingdom of God so that ultimately the Church could effectively live in and establish the Kingdom in the earth after their departure. Jesus trained His disciples to continue this mission until its ultimate conclusion. As the Kingdom mandate has been passed down through the generations, it has become diluted to the point that the message of the Church today often focuses on alternative religious themes rather than the Kingdom. We have the mandate to teach and advance the Kingdom in the earth. Much of the Church fails to understand God's kingdom principles and laws. Many do not have a kingdom mentality, especially Americans. In America, we don't have a king. In fact, we fought the Revolutionary War to be free from the king's oppression. And now, to show how we feel about kings, we name our dogs "King"!

The Kingdom of God is the Government of God

I am aware terminology such as "the Kingdom of God", "Kingdom theology", and "the gospel of the Kingdom" mean different things to different people. I want to be clear when I use this terminology it is understood to mean it is inclusive of the great revelation and truths given us in the New Testament. The Bible is a progressive revelation. Jesus is the express image of God's person, according to Hebrews 1:3, which means He is the perfect representation of God Himself. In addition, the New Testament epistles contribute as well to our fuller revelation of God. The message of the Kingdom, which can be referred to as the gospel of the Kingdom, should not be construed to mean a different message than was communicated by the Apostles and New Testament writers. Dr. Jack W. Hayford makes the following eloquent explanation:

> The synoptic Gospels and Acts make at least 20 direct references to the preaching of "the gospel of the Kingdom" from John the Baptist (Matt. 3.1-2), throughout Jesus' ministry (Mk. 1.14-15), in the disciples' ministry during Jesus' ministry (Lk. 9.1-2), and throughout Acts. Jesus prophesied this same message shall be taken to the ends of the world (Matt. 24.14), commissioning His disciples to do this and promising the Holy Spirit; power for the task (Mk. 16.15-18; Acts 1.3-8).

> It is clear that the early church proclaimed the same message Jesus preached, that is, "the gospel of the Kingdom of God" (Acts 8.12; 19.8; 20.25; 28.23, 30, 31). Also, they experienced the same confirming evidences present in His ministry.

> There is only one gospel: Jesus preached it, transmitted it to His disciples, and has committed it to His church. Paul warned against ever receiving any other gospel. "Any other" may be either a message of outright error or an argument for a diluted message, devoid of power though nominally Christian." (Spirit-Filled Life Bible 1469).

In Acts chapter twenty Paul addressed the elders of the church at Ephesus. He was determined to bypass Ephesus because he was in a hurry to get to Jerusalem for Pentecost. Instead of stopping at Ephesus he called for the elders to meet him at Miletus (Acts 20.16-17). This elders/pastors meeting is discussed through the rest of chapter twenty. As he spoke to them about his ministry he made the following statement in verses twenty-five and twenty-six, "And indeed, now I know that you all, among whom I have gone preaching the kingdom of God, will see my face no more. Therefore I testify to you this day that I am innocent of the blood of all men." He is addressing them in person because he doesn't expect to see them again. (v. 25). He explained that the ministry he received from the Lord Jesus was to testify to the gospel of the grace of God (v. 24) which he did throughout his missionary journeys, with the confirming signs and wonders which accompanied his preaching.

When Paul wrote to the Galatians he expressed shock that they had turned away from the gospel of the grace of God, "I marvel that you are turning away so soon from Him who called you in the grace of Christ, to a different gospel." (Gal. 1.6). Notice Paul made the point that the Galatians hadn't simply turned away from a doctrine. He said they were "turning away so soon from Him". When a person removes himself from the grace that is in Christ, he is turning away from Christ! This is strong! When grace is removed from the gospel, it is no longer the gospel at all. Paul is using "grace" and "gospel" interchangeably. Without grace there is no good news for a sinful world!

Now, let me refer back to Acts 20:24-25. Luke recorded that Paul said the ministry he received from the Lord Jesus was to testify to the gospel of the grace of God, then in the same breath continued, "And indeed, now I know that you all, among whom I have gone preaching the Kingdom of God, will see my face no more." In these two verses he connects the gospel of the grace of God to preaching the Kingdom of God! The gospel of the Kingdom is not, and should not be different than the gospel of the grace of God! There is only one gospel! The message of grace and faith connected to the gospel of the Kingdom in this progressive revelation! If the Kingdom is preached without grace and faith it is a perversion of the gospel. Kingdom living should not be legalistic and law-based. Grace and faith preached apart from Kingdom truth is incomplete. I want to be clear in my presentation that these truths are not exclusive of one another, and should not be interpreted as such.

The Kingdom of God is a vast subject and it is not my intent to do an exhaustive coverage of it here, but some definition and explanation is necessary. The Kingdom of God is His sovereign rule and reign. It is not a political system. It isn't a democracy that is ruled by the people, nor is it a bureaucracy which is ruled by a few. It is a theocracy which means it is ruled by God with Jesus as the King! This is the method God has chosen to govern His people. Kingdoms have rules and laws which govern them, just as natural realms have laws and rules which govern them.

I want to illustrate this with an elementary example that will help you to grasp this point. Imagine with me that you wanted to go explore the "kingdom" of outer space. For the sake of my illustration, I ask you to think of it in these terms. If you have enough money you can hire the Russians to fly you to the region we know as outer space. But before you go you must know the laws governing the realm. First, it's really cold up there! You must be clothed properly. Also, there is no oxygen so you must have a breathing apparatus. In order to survive in the realm, you must obey the laws governing it or you become a casualty of it! We all understand that laws are not subject to personal preference or debate. It doesn't matter if you believe in the laws or like the laws. In that kingdom you are subject to those laws. If you want to survive in that realm you must obey the laws governing it. Just as natural kingdoms or realms have laws governing them the Kingdom of God has laws governing it. Love is a law of the Kingdom; sowing and reaping is a law of the Kingdom as well as the law of faith to name a few. In the next chapter I will discuss further receiving by the law of faith, but for now I'll just say the sooner we understand and cooperate with the laws of the Kingdom, the sooner we will prosper in the

Kingdom!

Born Into the Kingdom

In John, chapter three, we are introduced to a man by the name of Nicodemus who was a ruler of the Jews. He was an influential and respected member of the Sanhedrin. As a Pharisee he was thoroughly trained in Jewish law and theology. We're told he came to Jesus by night. This could be interpreted in one of two ways; either because of embarrassment or fear of his peers. A glimpse of the repercussions of this action can be seen in the story of the healing of the man born blind, found in John chapter nine. As a result of the healing the Pharisees began to question the man's parents. The parents diverted the question to their son to allow him to answer for himself. Verse twenty-two tells us why, "His parents said these things because they feared the Jews, for the Jews had agreed already that if anyone confessed that he was Christ's, he would be put out of the synagogue." Perhaps it is for this reason Nicodemus came at night. Excommunication from the synagogue was serious. Jewish life revolved around their involvement in the Jewish worship system.

When Nicodemus saw Him, he called Him, "Rabbi", a tremendous term of respect from an older, well-respected man to give to Jesus who was much younger than he. He continued, "…we know that You are a teacher come from God; for no one can do these signs that You do unless God is with him." (v. 2). This is significant! It was the miraculous signs and wonders Jesus performed which caused Nicodemus to know He was from God! This is consistent with what we find in the New Testament and the early church record in the Book of Acts. The gospel was preached in power. The Apostle Paul said in 1 Corinthians 1:20, "For the Kingdom of God is not in word but in power." The great revival of Samaria from Acts 8:6-8 is just one example of this:

And the multitudes with one accord heeded the things spoken by Philip, hearing and seeing the miracles which he did. For unclean spirits, crying with a loud voice came out of many who were possessed; and many who were paralyzed and lame were healed. And there was great joy in that city.

The incorrect assumption which is common among many these days, that miracles have passed away, is a tremendous hindrance to advancing the Kingdom! Just as the supernatural power of God operating through Jesus caused Nicodemus to believe, our preaching should be confirmed by the supernatural power of God which would also cause people to believe.

Jesus' response to Nicodemus' comment is found in verse three, "Jesus answered and said to him, 'Most assuredly, I say to you, unless one is born again, he cannot see the Kingdom of God.'" The new birth is absolutely essential for entrance into the Kingdom of God. This could be rendered that one must be born from above. Unless one is born again, he cannot see or perceive the Kingdom. This coincides beautifully with 1 Corinthians 2:14, "But the natural man does not receive the things of the Spirit of God for they are foolishness to him; nor can he know them, because they are spiritually discerned." It was for this very reason Nicodemus did not understand Jesus' statement. Nicodemus said to Him, "How can a man be born when he is old? Can he enter a second time into his mother's womb and be born?" Jesus answered, "Most assuredly, I say to you, unless one is born of water and the Spirit, he cannot enter the Kingdom of God." (Jn. 3.4-5). Nicodemus had no understanding of what Jesus said; he immediately thought He was speaking of a natural, fleshly birth. Some have incorrectly thought the phrase, "born of water" refers to water baptism. If we look at this in context we can see Jesus was not referring to water baptism. In the same breath Jesus continued in verse six, "That which is born of the flesh is flesh, and that which is born of the Spirit is spirit." The phrase, "born of water" is simply a fleshly, natural birth. Andrew Wommack agrees:

> Being born of water is not speaking of water baptism as being essential for salvation. People were born again before they were baptized in water (Jn. 20:28 with Rom. 10:9). Cornelius and his household received the Holy Spirit (Acts 10:44-48) as evidenced by the gifts of the Holy Ghost, which Jesus said the world (lost) could not receive (Jn. 14:17) before they were baptized in water. (Gospels Edition 48).

Jesus marveled that Nicodemus, being a teacher of Israel, did not know these things (v. 10). Romans 10:9-10 tells us how to be born again: "that if you confess with your mouth the Lord Jesus and believe in your heart that God has raised Him from the dead, you will be saved. For with the heart one believes unto righteousness, and with the mouth confession is made unto salvation." God's gift of salvation is offered freely by God's grace, but it must be received by faith. Ephesians 2:8-9 brings this out, "For by grace you have been saved through faith, and that not of yourselves; it is the gift of God, not of works, lest anyone should boast." We know God is not willing that any should perish but that all should come to repentance (2 Pet. 3.9). God doesn't want anyone to perish, but there are those who do because they do not receive the free gift by faith. Titus 2:11, "For the grace of God that brings salvation has appeared to all men." Grace for salvation is for all men, but not all men receive it by faith.

A brief Greek word study sheds great light upon the fact that God is not only interested in our eternal destiny. In English the word salvation brings to mind eternal life, and going to heaven when we die. But in reality God has provided much more for us. The word "salvation" from Titus 2:11 comes from the Greek word *soterion* (Strong's

#4992). It is defined as rescue, deliverance, safety, liberation, release, preservation. A similar Greek word which is actually used more often in the New Testament is *soteria* (Strong's #4991), which is an all-inclusive word meaning, forgiveness, healing, prosperity, deliverance, safety, rescue, liberation and restoration. The salvation Jesus has provided for us is for the total man – spirit, soul and body! Forgiveness of our sins and the promise of everlasting life is awesome and more than we deserve, but is not all that has been provided. Jesus' substitutionary sacrifice has purchased our healing, deliverance, aid, rescue, safety and restoration for us. These all belong to us as born again believers! They have been made available by God's grace, but are now received by man's simple faith in God's redemptive plan.

Relationship with God

True Christianity is not simply behavior modification. The genuine Christian experience is not attained by living up to a certain standard, therefore appeasing an angry God who will weigh our good against our bad and if our good works exceed our bad works we will be granted acceptance. No, it is not possible to earn our salvation in any way. True relationship with God is something which is received, not something earned. By putting faith in Jesus' substitutionary sacrifice and accepting Jesus as our personal Savior we are changed on the inside. We literally become a new creature as is declared in 2 Corinthians 5:17, "Therefore, if anyone is in Christ, he is a new creation; old things have passed away; behold, all things have become new." We are not a refurbished or remodeled version of our old selves; no we become a new creature which didn't exist before! True Christianity does teach that we should live a good life. We should desire to live as holy as we can because we desire to be godly, but we should not live holy in an attempt to attain standing or relationship with Him. Holiness isn't a root of Christianity; it is a fruit of Christianity. Living a good life is the fruit of relationship with our God. This is important to understand because this is what distinguishes Christianity from other religions in this world.

In our politically correct culture tolerance is promoted. The ideology of political correctness is that religions or belief systems are equal. It doesn't matter what you believe, as long as you sincerely believe something. Relationship with God and our eternal salvation is all about Jesus. Some will say Jesus was a good example and that He is just one way to God and eternal life. But this is not what Jesus Himself taught: "Jesus said to him, I am the way, the truth and the life. No one comes to the Father Except through Me." (Jn. 14.6). Jesus is not a way, or just one of many. He is the only way to the Father! Acts chapter four records Peter's comments to the Sanhedrin after his arrest for the healing of the lame man at the gate of the Temple. While preaching about the name of Jesus Christ of Nazareth he said, "Nor is there salvation in any other, for there is no other name under heaven given among men by which we must be saved." (Acts 4.12).

A casual acknowledgment of God or of Jesus as His Son does not mean one has a true relationship with God. Genuine Christianity is more than merely acknowledging God exists. Notice what Jesus said in Matthew 7:21-23:

> Not everyone who says to Me, 'Lord, Lord,' shall enter the kingdom of heaven, but he who does the will of My Father in heaven. Many will say to Me in that day, 'Lord, Lord, have we not prophesied in Your name, cast out demons in Your name, and done many wonders in Your name?' And then I will declare to them, 'I never knew you; depart from Me, you who practice lawlessness!'

Jesus gave an example of people who claimed to know God but had no relationship with Him. Jesus said He never knew them. It wasn't a case of knowing Him at one time and then falling away. No, Jesus never knew them. They never had a true relationship with God even though they were attempting to do good works.

Another example to be considered is the religious leaders of Jesus' day. The scribes and Pharisees of Jesus' day lived up to a strict standard of outward, religious behavior. The way they dressed, and the rituals they kept were for the purpose of righteousness with God. But it was nothing but self-righteousness. Jesus castigated them severely in Matthew 23:27: "Woe to you, scribes and Pharisees, hypocrites! For you are like white washed tombs which indeed appear beautiful outwardly, but inside are full of dead men's bones and all uncleanness." It's possible to look good on the outside but be dead on the inside! Just because they observed religious rituals did not mean they had true relationship with God. Not every person who acknowledges God is real has a genuine relationship with Him. Scripture makes this clear in James 2:19, "You believe that there is one God. You do well. Even the demons believe – and tremble!" Demons believe in God, but they are not in relationship with Him because they do not submit to Jesus' lordship. To be in true relationship you have to believe and submit yourself to Him. You have to believe and be willing to act on what you believe.

Not long ago, at one of the Easter Sunday Chapel services at the Kyle Correctional Center where I am Chaplain, I preached the message and had given the altar call to which a large group of men responded for salvation and rededication. There were a group of volunteer ministers assisting me by praying with and for the men. There were several men waiting to be ministered to so I joined in praying with them. A young man came up to me and expressed his desire to be saved. I responded to him by simply asking him to answer a few questions before leading him in a sinner's prayer. I asked, "Do you believe in Jesus?" He said, "Yes". I asked, "Do you believe God sent Him?" "Yes" was his reply. I then asked, "Do you believe He died for your sins?" To which he responded, "Yes". I continued with my last question, "Do you believe God raised Him from the dead?" He then hesitated, and answered, "That's a little hard to believe." I explained to him he did need to believe in the resurrection in order to be saved. The Apostle Paul stated in 1 Corinthians 15:17, "And if Christ is not risen, your faith is futile; you are still in your sins!" It does matter what we believe and we must be willing to act on what we believe according to Romans 10:9-10: "that if you confess with your mouth the Lord Jesus and believe in your heart that God has raised Him from the dead, you will be saved. For with the heart one believes unto righteousness, and with the mouth confession is made unto salvation." With our heart we believe unto righteousness and with our mouth our confession of the Lordship of Jesus makes us alive unto God and gives us relationship as sons according to Galatians 4:4-7:

> But when the fullness of the time had come, God sent forth His Son, born of a woman, born under the law, to redeem those who were under the law, that we might receive the adoption as sons. And because you are sons, God has sent forth the Spirit of His Son into your hearts, crying out, "Abba, Father!" Therefore, you are no longer a slave but a son, and if a son, then an heir of God through Christ.

This is essential to relationship with God because man is born a sinner "...dead in trespasses and sins." (Eph. 2.1). Death means different things to different people. Some interpret death to mean you cease to exist, but in reality no one ceases to exist. Although our physical body dies and ultimately decays, our spirit and soul are eternal. For those of us who have been born again, we will be with the Lord. The natural man thinks of death as the end, but scripturally death means separation. An example of this is found in the experience of Adam and Eve. When they sinned they died spiritually. Their spirits did not cease to exist, but they were separated from God. They no longer had the life of God in them. After Adam and Eve's sin they produced children. Their sin nature was passed on to their children, who in turn passed the sin nature to theirs. In this manner the sin nature has passed to all men according to Romans 5:12, "Therefore, just as through one man sin entered the world, and death through sin, and thus death spread to all men, because all sinned." Because Jesus was born of a virgin He was not born with a sin nature. "Therefore the Lord Himself will give you a sign: behold, the virgin shall conceive and bear a Son and shall call His name Immanuel." (Isa. 7.14). Although this is a brief explanation it shows us why Jesus taught we must be "born again", because the spirit of every person who has not accepted Jesus is still dead.

Justification

We must have a working knowledge of the truth of our justification before God in order to live the victorious Christian life. I will begin this discussion with Romans 5:1, "Therefore, having been justified by faith, we have peace with God through our Lord Jesus Christ." An important aspect necessary for the believer to walk in victory is the peace we have with our God. It is impossible to imagine any believer experiencing total victory in their life without peace. This verse tells us this peace comes to us as a result of being justified by faith. Notice that it says, "having been justified". The word "justified" comes from the Greek work *dikaioo*, and is defined by Strong's Exhaustive Concordance as "to render just or innocent: free, justify, be righteous." (Strong's #1344). The first thing God does for the sinner at the new birth is to render him/her just or innocent in His sight! This is an instantaneous event. It is not something attained over time, or something one must grow into. It's not earned by our performance or good works. It is freely given as a benefit of our salvation. And is intended by God to be enjoyed by

His children. Peace with our God means there is no reason to struggle with a sense of guilt from the sins of our past. There is no need to carry excessive remorse for the mistakes and bad choices made in life prior to our new birth. Peace with God means we have been declared innocent. Therefore, there is no fear of punishment for the things we did which were deserving of punishment! The punishment we deserved was placed on Jesus as our substitute. As a result, justification is the announcement that the sinner is not guilty. In God's eyes the sins are gone, removed from us "As far as the east is from the west, so far has He removed our transgressions from us." (Ps. 103.12).

Remission of Sins

The benefits of this declaration of innocence is multifaceted. First, the sinner has sin's penalty remitted. The penalty for sin is death according to Romans 6:23, "For the wages of sin is death, but the gift of God is eternal life in Christ Jesus our Lord." Sin resulted in death spreading to all men. Romans 5:12, "Therefore, just as through one man sin entered the world and death through sin, and thus death spread to all men, because all sinned." This penalty was removed by the death of Christ on the cross. It was prophesied by Isaiah hundreds of years prior to His death.

> All we like sheep have gone astray; we have turned, every one, to his own way; and the Lord has laid on Him the iniquity of us all." He was oppressed and He was afflicted, yet He opened not His mouth; He was led as a lamb to the slaughter, and as a sheep before its shearers is silent, so He opened not His mouth. (Isa. 53.6-7).

The Apostle Peter made reference to it in his writings after Jesus' death, "Who Himself bore our sins in His own body on the tree, that we, having died to sins, might live for righteousness – by whose stripes you were healed." (1 Pet.

2.24). His reference was not only to the punishment for our sins, but included that Jesus had gone to the whipping post prior to hanging on the tree where He was beaten with stripes for our healing.

Restoration to Divine Favor

The second facet of blessing associated with our justification is restoration to divine favor. Not only were sinners experiencing death (separation from God) they had also lost His favor. I do not mean to suggest God had given up on man by turning His back on him. God had a plan of redemption from before the foundation of the world. God had long held a desire for His own special people, and Jesus' sacrifice enabled Him to present us to God as His own. This is also declared in the Apostle Peter's writings,

> But you are a chosen generation, a royal priesthood, a holy nation, His own special people, that you may proclaim the praises of Him who called you out of darkness into His marvelous light; who once were not a people but are now the people of God, who had not obtained mercy but now have obtained mercy. (1 Pet. 2.9-10).

Peter clearly said that once we were not a people, but we are now the people of God. We have been restored to favor with God as His own special people! The terminology chosen by the Apostle Paul for this special relationship with God is "sons". "For you are all sons of God through faith in Christ Jesus. For as many of you as were baptized into Christ have put on Christ." (Gal. 3.26-27). The Apostle John referenced this divine favor as being joyful fellowship with God in 1 John 1:3-4, "That which we have seen and heard we declare to you, that you also may have fellowship with us; and truly our fellowship is with the Father and with His Son Jesus Christ." This favor we have received truly makes our relationship with our God special! This desire of God was prophesied by Zephaniah and was expressed with terms of joyful favor and expression, "The Lord your God in your midst, the Mighty One, will save; He will rejoice over you with gladness, He will quiet you with His love, He will rejoice over you with singing." (Zeph. 3.17).

Imputed Righteousness

The third facet of blessing concerning our justification is imputed righteousness. Romans 3:21-22 tells us, "But now the righteousness of God apart from the law is revealed, being witnessed by the Law and the Prophets, even the righteousness of God through faith in Jesus Christ, to all and on all who believe. For there is no difference." Paul boldly declared there is now a manifested righteousness apart from the law. It was a bold statement which would have been unthinkable to the Jew. They had come to believe the only way to attain right standing or favor with God was to fulfill as much of the law as possible and to offer the prescribed sacrifices. Paul stated there is a righteousness revealed to us only available through faith in Christ. He referenced this in his letter to the Corinthians, "For He made Him who knew no sin to be sin for us, that we might become the righteousness of God in Him." (2 Cor. 5.21). Jesus didn't just take our sin; He was made to be sin for us. The sin of all mankind came on Jesus as He paid sin's penalty! And know this, He didn't die for the sins of the Church. He died for the sins of the world. A great exchange was made that day; He took our sin so we could receive His righteousness!

The Apostle John understood this and wrote boldly under the inspiration of the Holy Spirit, "Little children, let no one deceive you. He who practices righteousness is righteous, just as He is righteous." (1 Jn 3.7). Now look at 1 John 4:17, "Love has been perfected among us in this: that we may have boldness in the day of judgment; because as He is so are we in this world." A bold statement of truth, many do not understand today. We have been made the righteousness of God in Christ! This is what will enable us to be bold on the Day of Judgment. Know that we are declared innocent!

Thankfully, I have never had to face a judge in a courtroom to be sentenced for breaking a law or committing a crime. It is not possible for me to imagine I could possibly be at peace or be bold in that scenario knowing I was guilty! I can only imagine the fear, dread, and regret that would grip me as I would anticipate judgment being pronounced and being sentenced to receive punishment! According to the Apostle John's writing under the inspiration of the Holy Spirit our revelation is, as He is so are we in this world and we are the righteousness of God in Christ. This will enable us to be bold as we stand before God in the Day of Judgment! Rather than being sentenced for being guilty we will hear the breath-taking announcement that we are declared innocent! Praise God! Having been justified by faith in Jesus gives us peace. Peace with God to be enjoyed in our lives today and peace with God when we stand before Him on Judgment Day! What an empowering truth which enables us to enjoy victory today!

Become a Disciple

As essential as the new birth is to our relationship with God, it does not guarantee victory in life. There are many fine Christian people who love the Lord with all their heart who are living far below their rights and privileges in Christ. Being born again by placing faith in Jesus is not the end in our relationship with God, it is merely the beginning! God never intended for our spiritual development to end the moment it started. No, this is brought out clearly by Jesus when He gave the Great Commission to His disciples in Matthew 28:18-20:

And Jesus came and spoke to them, saying, 'All authority has been given to Me in heaven and on earth. Go therefore and make disciples of all the nations, baptizing them in the name of the Father and of the Son and of the Holy Spirit, teaching them to observe all things that I have commanded you; and lo, I am with you always, even to the end of the age.' Amen.

Notice the commission Jesus gave to the Church was not to go and make converts of all the nations, but rather to make disciples. Discipleship is a process of growth and maturity which takes place for the rest of our lives after having become a convert to Christianity. It's unfortunate that many need to be reminded of this. There are many who are saved and stuck and have not gone on to mature in Christ. Jesus said in John 8:31-32, "If you abide in My word, you are My disciples indeed. And you shall know the truth, and the truth shall make you free." Again, Jesus' words show that it is possible to be genuinely saved but not experience the freedom available to us. He gave us the key to experiencing freedom. He said, "If you abide in My word" – the King James Version uses the word "continue". True discipleship is more than simply being saved or born again. It is continuing, or abiding in the Word! The word "abide", or "continue" (KJV) comes from the Greek word *meno* and is defined by Strong's Exhaustive Concordance (Strong's #3306) as: "to stay, abide, continue, dwell, endure, be present, remain, stand, or tarry". To abide in God's Word means to stay in the Word, to dwell, to remain in the Word, or to stand or tarry in it. As an example, think about your home. The place where you live is your dwelling, or your abode. The place where you abide reflects who you are. We customize and decorate our homes according to our own desires and particular tastes. I may not even know you personally, but if you were to invite me to your home, the moment I walk in I can begin to learn some things about you.

As an example, my wife has decorated our home beautifully. We have Christian and patriotic symbols in our front room, as well as photos of our travels, some of my woodworking projects throughout the house and pictures of our grandkids on the walls. Our home truly reflects who we are, our deep love for God, our love for our family, as well as honor and respect for our nation. Likewise, when you truly abide in God's Word, by making it your dwelling place, by falling in love with Jesus and His Word, it affects you. It begins to shape your life, your personality and desires. A genuine disciple begins to be a disciplined one who becomes like his master. A true disciple of Jesus doesn't want to look and act like the world. In fact, a true disciple is affected by the truth and the truth begins to make him or her free! There should be a difference between us and the world, and one of the main differences which should be noticeable to all is that we are free! Free of worry! Free of fear! Free of life-controlling habits and addictions. Amen!

Rooted and Grounded

True discipleship is obtained by establishing a solid foundation on the Word of God. A beautiful word picture was used by the Old Testament prophet Jeremiah:

> Blessed is the man who trusts in the Lord, and whose hope is the Lord. For he shall be like a tree planted by the waters, which spreads out its roots by the river, and will not fear when heat comes; but its leaf will be green, and will not be anxious in the year of drought, nor will cease from yielding fruit. (Jer. 17.7-8).

What a beautiful picture of the life God desires for us! The Prophet said the man who trusts in the Lord would be like a tree planted by the rivers of water, whose roots run deep by the river. This speaks to me of a strong foundation. This is a prosperous, healthy, well-provided for tree! It is so solidly connected to the water source that there is no fear or anxiety when heat comes or in a year of drought. Not only that, but he said this is a tree which is fruitful even in the year of drought! This is an amazing description of what our lives can resemble when we are rooted and grounded in God through His Word. There can be no substitute for the Bible for establishing a solid foundation in the life of a disciple. You just can't overstate the value of the Word of God in our lives.

Many years ago I worked with my dad for a construction company in Colorado. The contractor was developing a mine site in the mountains above Parachute, Colorado. My dad and I were working down in the Colorado River Valley developing a gravel pit for the same contractor. We had to clear many Cottonwood trees away so that the overburden topsoil could be removed to get to the river rock beneath which would be crushed into gravel. Normally we would cut down trees with chainsaws and then skid them away. But one particular time I watched as my dad was operating a very large, track-mounted Caterpillar backhoe. He reached up with the large, heavy boom and began to push on a Cottonwood tree toward its top. I watched as he pushed on the tree to rock it back and forth loosening it from the roots. Finally, after enough force was applied by the powerful machine, he pushed the tree over to the ground. When he did, it pulled up a huge root ball at the base of the tree. The root system under those large trees are enormous! It left a crater in the soil about the size of a car! The roots of a Cottonwood tree run deep into the earth – well into the water table where it is well-nourished and supplied. Our "roots" in the Christian life should be solidly established in the Word of God yet often believers are too shallow in their foundation.

In contrast to the Cottonwood trees I was familiar with in Colorado are the types of trees I encountered in the tropics. Several years after my experience in the gravel pit, I joined the United States Air Force in 1987. My first duty assignment was Clark Air Base Republic of the Philippines. When I arrived at Clark Air Base, I was surprised by the trees I saw. There were trees with vines hanging from them that looked like roots coming from their branches. They would actually hang to the ground and take root in the soil. In addition, I noticed roots extending from the base of the tree along the top of the ground far from the trunk. I had never seen such a tree. I thought to myself, "We don't have trees like this in Colorado!"

I had my first experience with a tropical typhoon while I was stationed there. I remember the weather service began to broadcast warnings of an approaching storm. About twenty-four hours before the storm was to hit, we were released from our work assignments to secure our homes and families. They were predicting Clark Air Base would sustain a direct hit from the storm. We were warned not to be lulled into complacency by the calm "eye of the storm". As forecast, the storm passed directly over Clark Air Base. The wind blew with great force. Trees and branches were destroyed. Power lines toppled. There was damage to houses. We lost power and water supply. Then it became calm as the eye passed over. Before long the back side of the storm slammed into us.

When it was all over and it became safe to drive, I was curious to see the damage. Clark Air Base had a large, well-manicured golf course. I drove by it and saw as many as one hundred trees had been blown down and destroyed by the storm! As I looked, I noticed there was no crater left in the soil from the root ball like I had seen in the gravel pit in Colorado. The trees had only pulled up a few inches of topsoil in a wide circumference of the base. Their root system was shallow. They had little resistance to the wind speeds. It left a bare spot on the ground. Colossians 2:6-7 tells us, "As you therefore have received Christ Jesus the Lord, so walk in Him, rooted and built up in Him and established in the faith, as you have been taught, abounding in it with thanksgiving." The only way to be rooted, built up and established in faith is to "study to show yourself approved unto God" (2 Tim. 2.15). This will enable us to establish a solid foundation in our relationship with God upon which we can build our lives.

Our forgiveness, justification, and imputed righteousness are vast subjects that would require a lengthy discourse to cover adequately. I don't mean to diminish their value by not exploring them in detail. I simply want to establish the fact that everything we need for life and godliness has been made available to us, and in the next chapter I will discuss accessing the grace of God by the law of faith and enforcing the victory that has already been won. I will let it suffice to conclude this chapter with comments from Dr. Myles Munroe:

> A pardon declares its recipient to be as innocent as if the offense never occurred. Once a person is pardoned, the government returns his or her passport, and from that moment forward that person is free to travel, work, engage in business, buy and sell and enjoy all other citizen rights and privileges without limitation. A pardon justifies and reestablishes a person's righteousness in the eyes of the law.

> That is what Jesus did for all of us on the cross. His death and shed blood bought our pardon and made us righteous in the eyes of God once more. Our Kingdom citizenship and rights were restored, and we were positioned once again as recipients and heirs of all God's promises. (Rediscovering the Kingdom 99).

3 RECEIVING FROM GOD THROUGH THE LAW OF FAITH

In the previous chapter, I pointed out that John the Baptist and Jesus preached the good news of the gospel of the Kingdom of God. Their message was adopted and proclaimed by the early church in the Book of Acts. Much of the modern church has departed from the original mandate and now simply preaches the good news of Heaven. They tell people to put their faith in Jesus for salvation and then focus on Heaven as their goal and destination. As a result of this inaccurate approach, many Christians are saved and stuck!

Christians who make Heaven their goal and destination become professional pew-sitters who sit back and do nothing for the Kingdom. The goal of our salvation should not simply be getting our ticket punched so we can go to Heaven and escape Hell. The goal of the Christian life is to be like Jesus, to be conformed into His image. Romans 8:29 tells us, "For whom He foreknew, He also predestined to be conformed to the image of His Son, that He might be the firstborn among many brethren".

Paul told us God's people should undergo a

transformational process in their character and become like Jesus. With Jesus as our Lord and Savior we get to go to Heaven and no longer need to focus primarily on Heaven as our goal. The promise of Heaven is a comfort in difficult times, but it is not and should not be the focus of our preaching. It is common in many churches, week after week, for pastors to preach salvation sermons to saved people but fail to expound on the many other truths which will make them free. Scripture doesn't promise that Jesus would rescue us from a world on the brink of overcoming us. No, it says in Him we should overcome the world! Jesus said, "These things I have spoken to you, that in Me you may have peace. In the world you will have tribulation; but be of good cheer, I have overcome the world." (Jn. 16.33). 1 John 5:4 tells us, "For whatever is born of God overcomes the world. And this is the victory that has overcome the world – our faith."

This means when we live, think, and act like Kingdom citizens, we can experience success, victory, and fruitfulness! Not only in Heaven after we die, but presently in this life as well! We can avail ourselves of our Kingdom citizenship and all its blessings, rights, and benefits to rise above our circumstances. Kingdom living does not sit back in submission and defeat. Kingdom living moves forward with confidence, advancing forcefully in wisdom, power and boldness! Jesus preached the gospel of the Kingdom of Heaven, but His message had little to do with going to Heaven. In fact, He preached the opposite; Heaven was coming to earth. He taught the disciples to pray, "Our Father which art in heaven, hallowed be Thy name. Thy kingdom come, Thy will be done on earth as it is in heaven." (Matt. 6.9-10 KJV).

The idea of reigning in life as presented by the apostle in Romans 5:17 wasn't a new concept. It was, in fact, in the heart of God from the beginning as demonstrated in Genesis 1:26, "Then God said, 'Let Us make man in Our image, according to Our likeness; let them have dominion over the fish of the sea, over the birds of the air, and over the cattle, over all the earth and over every creeping thing that creeps on the earth."'

> God created man because He desired someone to rule over the physical realm He had created. The King James Version of the Bible uses the word dominion which is related to the word domain. Human beings were created to exercise dominion over the earth and all its creatures. Earth is the domain of humanity's rulership. (Munroe, "Rediscovering the Kingdom" 49).

It is important to note the New Testament revelation concerning the position and authority given to believers through our Lord Jesus Christ. After Jesus was raised from the dead, the Bible says God highly exalted Him to a position of honor at His right hand and gave Him a name which is above every name (Phil. 2.9-10). Now notice what Ephesians 1:17-21 says:

> ...that the God of our Lord Jesus Christ, the Father of glory, may give to you the spirit of wisdom and revelation in the knowledge of Him, the eyes of your understanding being enlightened; that you may know what is the hope of His calling, what are the riches of the glory of His inheritance in the saints, and what is the exceeding greatness of His power toward us who believe, according to the working of His mighty power which He worked in Christ when He raised Him from the dead and seated Him at His right hand in the heavenly places, far above all principality and power and might and dominion, and every name that is named, not only in this age but also in that which is to come.

God seated Jesus in the highest position in the universe and made Him head over all things. Notice He's not just seated above principality, power, might, and dominion; He's seated "far above" all principality, power, might and dominion (v. 21)! Let's understand how Jesus' seating in the highest position in the universe affects us as believers. God "… raised us up together, and made us sit together in the heavenly places in Christ Jesus". (Eph. 2.6). Believers are seated together with Christ in heavenly places! Our joint seating with Christ is "far above" all of the demonic realm. This is positional truth. Our position with Christ is a position of honor, authority, and triumph – not failure and defeat! As believers, being seated with Christ is a part of our inheritance now. We don't have to wait until we get to heaven to enjoy it! Notice these verses are written in past tense. It has already been given to us. We can reign in life now if we will exercise the authority which has been given to us. The basic premise is our position as believers is one of joint seating with Christ. This may not always be our circumstance in the physical realm, but it is always our position in the spiritual realm!

If we want to rise above our circumstances, we must take advantage of our position! As believers we won't experience the victory if we don't understand what belongs to us. We cannot possess what we do not know. "And you shall know the truth, and the truth shall make you free." (Jn. 8.32). Hosea 4:6 says, "My people are destroyed for lack of knowledge." The world says, "What you don't know won't hurt you." I say, "What you don't know is killing you"! Andrew Wommack has this to say about Ephesians 2:6:

The terms 'made us sit" (v. 6), 'raised' (Ephesians 1:20; v. 6), and 'quickened' (vv.1, 5), are all terms that are in the aorist tense, which indicates something that God has already accomplished in Christ and not something that is off in the future. To be raised up together with Christ and made to sit together "in heavenly places" indicate not only location but also a position of authority. It is because of our position of being raised up with Christ that all things, including the demonic realm, are put under our feet (Ephesians 1:22-23). We are to exercise this authority in this present evil age through preaching the gospel, including healing the sick and casting out devils. (Galatians, Ephesians and Colossians 1103).

The Kingdom of God is advanced on a principle of faith. As we embrace the will of God the Kingdom is established. I want to discuss our role as believers in this. Matthew 11:12 says, "And from the days of John the Baptist until now the Kingdom of Heaven suffers violence, and the violent take it by force." Today, as in the days of John the Baptist, Satan is opposing the preaching of the gospel. Only those who are violently resolved to receive God's best will have God's best.

When John the Baptist came on the scene in the power of the Spirit preaching faith in the coming Messiah, multitudes who were not seeking God began flocking into the wilderness to be baptized, confess their sin and put faith in the Messiah. They were "violently resolved" in their zeal and forcefully pressing into the Kingdom. This violent resolve is the missing ingredient in many people's lives today. A certain amount of violence is involved in the Kingdom. We must take an aggressive, offensive position in our Christian walk as we take hold of the will of God. The Kingdom of God is not something we enter into with an uncommitted, passive attitude.

Rather, we must take hold of the truth and not let go! The violent take it by force with an attitude that will not be denied! Often I encounter people who say, "I'm just standing in faith". What they mean, essentially, is "I'm just patiently waiting on God." That is not standing in faith! Patience is a fruit of the Spirit and there is value in having patience in our lives, but we must understand faith isn't passively waiting; it is actively believing and speaking God's Word.

Notice Luke 16:16, "The law and the prophets were until John. Since that time the Kingdom of God has been preached, and everyone is pressing into it." This demonstrates that advancing the Kingdom is a result of preaching and pressing into it. The Kingdom of God must be preached with a spiritual passion! Preachers have a tremendous responsibility to preach the gospel of the Kingdom. It must be understood by our ministers in order to present it properly. The Church has a responsibility as well. Spiritual passivity, the attitude "whatever will be, will be", will not advance the Kingdom! The will of God is not automatic; we must take hold of the will of God and do it. God is not working in our lives independent of us; we must cooperate with Him by faith.

I need to explain the terminology I'm using. When I speak of being forceful, violent and pressing in, I do not mean we force God to save, forgive, or heal. Nor do I mean we are somehow applying pressure on God in an attempt to persuade Him or talk Him into the notion of being good, to move on our behalf or bless us. I simply mean that we must use our faith and believe what God has already done for us. We use faith which cooperates with God by responding positively to what He has already provided by taking hold of the will of God by believing His Word and acting on it. We use our faith to enforce Jesus' victory and free people from Satan's dominion and power. The Bible clearly says, "He has delivered us from the power of darkness and conveyed us into the kingdom of the Son of His love." (Col. 1.13). The moment we were born again we were made alive and transferred into the Kingdom of God as citizens of His kingdom. (Phil. 3.20).

Victory over the devil was won by Jesus on the cross. We don't have to defeat him; we simply have to enforce what has already been won! We enforce the victory by using the name of Jesus to stand and take the dominion He has provided for the Church! The basic premise is we are not headed toward a victory – we are coming from a victory! We don't have to win the victory – we enforce it! To maintain our victorious position requires a "violent" type of faith -- a forceful type of faith!

As an illustration of this, let's look at an ancient military strategy. This strategy doesn't apply as much to modern warfare with aircraft, missiles, and smart-bomb technology, but from the ancient foot soldier mentality, military strategy was to gain control of the high ground. The idea was, it is much easier to hold a position than to defeat it. When entrenched in strategic high ground, the position could be defended with a relatively small number of troops compared to the number required to overcome it.

This should be our mentality! We're not the defeated trying to win! We're not the sick trying to get healed! With this understanding we can stand confidently on the Word with assurance; not attempting to win the victory but rather enforcing the victory already won by Jesus! In Matthew 16:18 (KJV) Jesus said, "I will build My church and the gates of hell will not prevail against it." He didn't leave us powerless and defeated. He made us triumphant and victorious! For too long the Church has had the mentality of a defensive position against the onslaught of the enemy, just trying to hold on until Jesus catches us away. No! That's not our position! The Church should be advancing forcefully against the gates of hell and those gates cannot stop the advance!

The Shunammite Woman

To maintain our victorious position requires a violent, forceful faith which will not be denied. If this is an accurate scriptural position for us to embrace, there must be examples of it from Scripture. Indeed, there are. I want to examine a few. I will begin first from an Old Testament example in

2 Kings 4:8-37.

> Now it happened one day that Elisha went to Shunem, where there was a notable woman, and she persuaded him to eat some food. So it was, as often as he passed by, he would turn in there to eat some food. And she said to her husband, "Look now, I know that this is a holy man of God, who passes by us regularly. Please, let us make a small upper room on the wall; and let us put a bed for him there, and a table and a chair and a lampstand; so it will be, whenever he comes to us, he can turn in there." (vv. 8-10).

Let's understand the scenario, this Shunammite woman was accustomed to Elisha regularly visiting their community. Paraphrased, she was saying, "Since the Prophet is coming by every so often, let's build him a room up on the wall so when he comes, he'll have a place to stay." She's not hoping to get anything from the man of God, she's just wanting to bless him. She's wanting to show hospitality to the prophet. Verse eleven and following continues…

> And it happened one day that he came there, and he turned in to the upper room and lay down there. Then he said to Gehazi his servant, "Call this Shunammite woman." When he had called her, she stood before him. And he said to him, "Say now to her, 'Look, you have been concerned for us with all this care. What can I do for you? Do you want me to speak on your behalf to the king or to the commander of the army?'" She answered, "I dwell among my own people." (vv. 11-13).

In other words, she's saying that's not why she did it. She didn't build this room so she could use his influence or his power to make something happen for her. She was happy to dwell with her own people. This is showing us the motive of her heart. Verse fourteen continues, "What then is to be done for her?" And Gehazi answered, "Actually, she has no son, and her husband is old."

In order to fully appreciate this, we need to understand her circumstance. Here's a woman whose husband was old and they were without a son to carry on their posterity. In those days all the inheritance would go to a son. A son would ensure protection and provision for her in her old age. We don't have all the detail we'd like but this couple had probably been trying, believing and wanting children for a long time. Verses fifteen and sixteen tell us, "So he said, 'Call her.' When he had called her, she stood in the doorway. Then he said, 'About this time next year you shall embrace a son.' And she said, 'No, my lord. Man of God, do not lie to your maidservant!'" We don't know how old she was. We know her husband was already old, but it sounds like this is desperation in her voice, like she had given up hope of having a son. It's almost like she is having a hard time believing this. Continuing in verse seventeen and eighteen: "But the woman conceived, and bore a son when the appointed time had come, of which Elisha had told her. And the child grew. Now it happened one day that he went out to his father, to the reapers." (2 Kings 4.18). Again, it would be nice to have more detail here. I don't know how many years have passed, so we don't know the boy's age. We know the child grew and he was out in the field helping his father. And while he's out working in the field, something happens to him; possibly a heat stroke or a heat-related illness as he's working in the field.

The next two verses: "And he said to his father, 'My head, my head!' So he said to a servant, 'Carry him to his mother.' When he had taken him and brought him to his mother, he sat on her knees till noon, and then died." (vv. 19-20). This boy had been working in the field and was overcome by the heat. The father told a servant, "Carry him to his mother." The servant took him into the house and he died in his mother's lap!

> And she went up and laid him on the bed of the man of God, shut the door upon him, and went out. Then she called to her husband, and said, "Please send me one of the young men and one of the donkeys, that I may run to the man of God and come back." So he said, "Why are you going to him today? It is neither the New Moon nor the Sabbath." (vv.21-23).

Notice what she didn't say, "Oh God, our child has died. Oh no, what are we going to do?" No, that's not what the Bible says. When asked by her husband, she replied, "It is well." I don't mean to criticize anyone, but most people sense no responsibility in a tragedy like this. Many would have no criticism for this woman at all if she were overcome with sadness and grief.

I'm using this as an example of a woman who has a violent resolve that will not be defeated. Here's a woman who did not have all the benefits we have. Jesus had not yet been to the cross. The devil had not yet been defeated. She was not born again. This was a woman who was not Spirit-filled and did not have the Bible, especially the New Testament with Paul's revelation as we have. This is an example of an Old Testament woman with a violent resolve that would not quit and would not be denied. Let's read on…

> Then she saddled a donkey, and said to her servant, "Drive, and go forward; do not slacken the pace for me unless I tell you." And so she departed, and went to the man of God at Mount Carmel. So it was, when the man of God saw her afar off, that he said to his servant Gehazi, "Look, the Shunammite woman! Please run now to meet her, and say to her, 'Is it well with you? Is it well with your husband? Is it well with the child?'" And she

answered, "It is well." Now when she came to the man of God at the hill, she caught him by the feet, but Gehazi came near to push her away. But the man of God said, "Let her alone; for her soul is in deep distress, and the Lord has hidden it from me, and has not told me." (vv. 24-27).

What?! Her soul is in *deep* (my emphasis) distress? We weren't told that. Up until this point, we wouldn't even have known that she was in deep distress by her actions if the scripture hadn't told us. Because, all she said was, "It is well." The woman's boy had just died in her lap that day! Her soul is in deep distress but she's not acting upon what's happening in her soul. Many people feel completely justified in acting on their feelings. If they're mad, throw the chair. If they hurt, kick the dog, or punch the wall!

> Now when she came to the man of God at the hill, she caught him by the feet, but Gehazi came near to push her away. But the man of God said, "Let her alone; for her soul is in deep distress, and the LORD has hidden it from me, and has not told me." So she said, "Did I ask a son of my lord? Did I not say, 'Do not deceive me'?" Then he said to Gehazi, "Get yourself ready, and take my staff in your hand, and be on your way. If you meet anyone, do not greet him; and if anyone greets you, do not answer him; but lay my staff on the face of the child." And the mother of the child said, "As the LORD lives, and as your soul lives, I will not leave you." So he arose and followed her." (vv. 27-30).

She wasn't having this. She was not about to leave without the man of God! So he arose and followed her.

> "Now Gehazi went on ahead of them, and laid the staff on the face of the child; but there was neither voice nor hearing. Therefore, he went back to meet him, and told

him, saying, 'The child has not awakened.'" (v. 31).

Now notice what Elisha didn't say, "Well, I guess we just have to give up then because if it was meant to be, it would be. Let the will of God be done." Unfortunately, there are people who think this way and just accept it as though there is nothing that can be done. Our attitude should be that the first report is not the last report! There was a violent resolve in this woman and there was a violent resolve in the man of God!

> When Elisha came into the house, there was the child, lying dead on his bed. He went in therefore, shut the door behind the two of them, and prayed to the LORD. And he went up and lay on the child, and put his mouth on his mouth, his eyes on his eyes, and his hands on his hands; and he stretched himself out on the child, and the flesh of the child became warm. He returned and walked back and forth in the house, and again went up and stretched himself out on him; then the child sneezed seven times, and the child opened his eyes. And he called Gehazi and said, "Call this Shunammite woman." So he called her. And when she came in to him, he said, "Pick up your son." So she went in, fell at his feet, and bowed to the ground; then she picked up her son and went out. (vv. 32-37).

This powerful story illustrates so well what I am presenting about laying hold of the will of God and not letting go. It depicts how the man of God and this woman expected a miracle to establish the will of God in their lives. It's an example of a violent type of faith…a forceful type of faith that leads one out of defeat and into victory. I'm telling you that an active, energetic faith will lead you out of defeat and into victory. God wants you to win and He's established it so you can win.

One last thing. This story could have had a different ending. We could have read how the boy died and sad to say they had his funeral the next day. You know why it didn't end like that? Because, here was a woman who wouldn't give up and wouldn't accept defeat. I believe this is the missing ingredient in many Christians today. Now, I want to examine a few New Testament examples which illustrate the need for applying the laws of faith.

The Law of Faith

Remember, the Kingdom operates according to spiritual law. Let's notice Romans 3:27 uses this exact terminology, "Where is boasting then? It is excluded. By what law? Of works? No, but by the law of faith." The subject of faith, as the subject of the Kingdom, is vast and I will not deal with it in detail but some explanation is necessary. If the only verse in the Bible on faith was Hebrews 11:6, "But without faith it is impossible to please Him, for he who comes to God must believe that He is, and that He is a rewarder of those who diligently seek Him.", this would be reason enough to want to major on the subject of faith. Thankfully we have many, many verses and chapters dedicated to helping us understand the importance of our faith in God.

The author of the book of Hebrews explains, "God, who at various times and in various ways spoke in time past to the fathers by the prophets, has in these last days spoken to us by His Son, whom He has appointed heir of all things, through whom also He made the worlds;". This verse is simply telling us God has dealt with men in different ways throughout human history. Although the way God has dealt with man through the years has changed, one thing never has changed and that is the way man approaches God.

Man has always approached God by faith and always will approach God by faith. This is illustrated beautifully for us in the eleventh chapter of Hebrews. This chapter has been referred to as God's great Hall of Fame, or Hall of Faith. The author reviews many Old Testament saints who used their faith in triumphant experiences which stand as great testaments to help us see what faith can do. These are raised as examples of faith which pleased God. These saints didn't have the benefits available to them that we enjoy today. Jesus had not yet been to the cross, the devil had not yet been defeated, the wonderful New Testament truths had not yet been recorded, and they were able to stand victorious. How much more should we be able to reign in life by our faith?

The Christian life is to be regulated and conducted by faith, as opposed to external and outward appearances based on physical sight. Thus the reason 2 Corinthians 5:7 tells us, "For we walk by faith, not by sight." This is a simple principle most of us find difficult to follow because most of us are more dominated by our senses than we are our faith. This is a challenge for all of us, but we are commanded to learn it. The Apostle Paul spoke practically to the Corinthians concerning the use of faith in 2 Corinthians 4:7-18:

> But we have this treasure in earthen vessels, that the excellence of the power may be of God and not of us. We are hard-pressed on every side, yet not crushed; we are perplexed, but not in despair; persecuted, but not forsaken; struck down, but not destroyed— always carrying about in the body the dying of the Lord Jesus, that the life of Jesus also may be manifested in our body. For we who live are always delivered to death for Jesus' sake, that the life of Jesus also may be manifested in our mortal flesh. So then death is working in us, but life in you.
>
> And since we have the same spirit of faith, according to what is written, "I believed and therefore I spoke," we

also believe and therefore speak, knowing that He who raised up the Lord Jesus will also raise us up with Jesus, and will present us with you. For all things are for your sakes, that grace, having spread through the many, may cause thanksgiving to abound to the glory of God.

Therefore, we do not lose heart. Even though our outward man is perishing, yet the inward man is being renewed day by day. For our light affliction, which is but for a moment, is working for us a far more exceeding and eternal weight of glory, while we do not look at the things which are seen, but at the things which are not seen. For the things which are seen are temporary, but the things which are not seen are eternal.

The context of the chapter is troubles, tests, and trials. It is important to understand that living by faith does not mean freedom from trouble! In fact, it might be more accurate to say, "When we make the decision to live by faith, let the problems begin." The reason I say this is because we have a real spiritual enemy. Everyday there is a battle raging for our lives. Many people, including some Christians, sad to say, have a humanistic view of life. A view which denies the existence of the spiritual realm. They view everything that happens from a natural standpoint with natural explanations. If you view everything from a natural standpoint and live according to the flesh, thinking only of the flesh, that is called carnality. The humanists don't acknowledge God or the spiritual realm. They believe everything is natural or physical, therefore everything has a natural or physical cause. God is trying to influence people and draw them to Himself, and Satan is in an all-out war attempting to deceive the hearts of men so he can kill, steal, and destroy (Jn. 10.10). Many people don't recognize the importance of their daily choices. Our choices determine whether God is able to move with blessing flowing into our lives or whether Satan can dominate our lives. There is a war raging, but we have much to do with the outcome of it in our life.

When Paul spoke of faith in 2 Corinthians chapter four it was in the context of troubles. Later, in the same letter, he spoke of being beaten, imprisoned, shipwrecked, robbed; of experiencing weariness, hunger, cold and nakedness. Paul was no stranger to persecution and troubles! But I want to point out his attitude toward them. In 2 Corinthians 4:17 he called them a light affliction: "For our light affliction, which is but for a moment, is working for us a far more exceeding and eternal weight of glory." Paul was so completely focused on eternal values that temporal things just could not compare! Problems are real, but they should not be the focus of our attention.

He went on to say in verse eighteen, "while we do not look at the things which are seen, but at the things which are not seen. For the things which are seen are temporary, but the things which are not seen are eternal." What? He said to look at the things which aren't seen. How can you look at that which is not seen? Through the eye of faith! Problems can cause discouragement and frustration. Don't let discouragement rob you of your faith! We have a powerful God who has made His power available to us, and there are no impossible situations. All things are possible to those who believe. Remember, you are a believer, not a doubter! The critics say, faith people believe that living by faith means we won't have problems. No, living by faith does not mean we won't have problems, but living by faith means we can overcome every one of them!

Faith Believes and Speaks

This is what Paul brought out in this passage. Notice again what he said in 2 Corinthians 4:13-15:

And since we have the same spirit of faith, according to

what is written, 'I believed and therefore I spoke' we also believe and therefore speak, knowing that He who raised up the Lord Jesus will also raise us up with Jesus, and will present us with you. For all things are for your sakes, that grace, having spread through the many, may cause thanksgiving to abound to the glory of God.

That's incredible! In the midst of problems, he wrote of exercising faith to make him victorious! He didn't pray one of those faithless, passive prayers, "Lord, just please help me to accept this." No. His attitude was he could turn it around with his faith. Notice he said in verse thirteen, "since we have the same spirit of faith". He didn't say we're trying to have the same faith or praying for, or hoping to get, the same spirit of faith. He said we "have the same spirit of faith." What kind of faith is that? The kind of faith which believes and therefore speaks. Don't tell me we can't speak our faith in the midst of problems! I want to point out real Bible faith believes what God said in His Word. That's where faith begins, by believing the Bible with the heart. Then you must act on what you believe by saying it with your mouth. Faith has two parts, believing and speaking.

Jesus and the Fig Tree

Jesus taught us about faith. Some of the greatest things we know about faith come directly from His teachings. As an example, on the day after His triumphal entry into Jerusalem, walking from Bethany into Jerusalem, Mark 11:13-14 records the following:

And seeing from afar a fig tree having leaves, He went to see if perhaps He would find something on it. When He came to it, He found nothing but leaves, for it was not the season for figs. In response Jesus said to it, "Let no one eat fruit from you ever again." And His disciples heard it.

Jesus taught and exemplified the power of words spoken in faith. Someone may argue, "Yes, but He was God!" It is true that Jesus was and is God, but Jesus stripped Himself of divine privilege and humbled Himself as a man. Notice Philippians 2:6-7 (Weymouth), "From the beginning He had the nature of God. Yet He did not regard equality with God as something at which He should grasp. Nay, He stripped Himself of His glory, and took on Him the nature of a bondservant by becoming a man like other men." This means, He ministered on the earth as a man. He operated according to the laws of the Kingdom, faith being one of those laws.

Verse fourteen says, "In response Jesus said to it…" Jesus responded to a tree! This means the tree was communicating that it had figs because it had leaves. Andrew Wommack agrees:

> Why would Jesus curse this fig tree? The scripture gives no explanation of this. However, it is a fact that a fig tree should have figs by the time the leaves are evident. The fig tree actually produces green figs before the leaves appear and if no figs are produced by that time, then that tree will not have any figs that year. Therefore, this fig tree was professing something that it didn't have even though it was still too early for figs. It was hypocritical. It is probable that this hypocrisy in nature occasioned Jesus' curse just as hypocritical people suffered Jesus' harshest rebukes (Mt. 23). It is also possible that Jesus knew this action would gain the attention of His disciples and He would therefore use it to teach them a lesson on faith. (Gospels Edition 362).

This was not a case of Jesus simply using His power to kill a tree. No, He used this as an object lesson to teach how faith works. Just as this tree was communicating, other things communicate as well. Circumstances can tell you, you have failed. Your body can tell you, you are not healed, etc. We must learn from Jesus' example to respond to these things in faith! Another important detail to notice is it says, "His disciples heard it." (v. 14). This wasn't a silent request; He didn't pray about it and ask God to curse the tree. He spoke, out loud, to the tree! I can imagine the disciples saying, "What is He doing? Our Master has lost it. He's speaking to trees!" I believe Jesus used this as an object lesson. He took this opportunity to teach and exemplify faith.

After spending the day in Jerusalem, they returned to Bethany for the night. The next morning, they passed by and saw the tree dried up from the roots (v. 20). Verse twenty-one records Peter's response, "And Peter, remembering, said to Him, "Rabbi, look! The fig tree which You cursed has withered away." They saw the fig tree had dried up from the roots. This is significant for us to understand – the words went straight to the root! Words spoken in faith go to the root of the problem! The problem/circumstance may not change instantly, but if the roots are dead, the tree is dead. I have cut down trees before. When they hit the ground, they don't look dead. They are still green; they are still moist. They sit there, seeming to say, "I'm not dead! I'm not dead!" But just wait a day or two. The same tree which doesn't look dead today will look dead tomorrow because I promise you, if it is severed from the roots, its dead. It's just a matter of time; if the root is dead the tree will die!

Faith is Voice-Activated

Then Jesus proceeded to give the outstanding teaching on what faith is:

So Jesus answered and said to them, "Have faith in God. For assuredly, I say to you, whoever says to this mountain, 'Be removed and be cast into the sea,' and does not doubt in his heart, but believes that those things he says will be done, he will have whatever he says. Therefore I say to you, whatever things you ask when you pray, believe that you receive them, and you will have them". (Mk. 11.22-24).

Faith is released by speaking words. Speaking is emphasized three times in verse twenty-three. We are commanded by Jesus to believe what we say will come to pass! We are to believe in the power of our words. Failure to believe in the power of words won't keep it from working. The verse ends with, "he will have whatever he says." If we speak faith-filled words that are in line with God's Word we will have the positive results which follow. However, if we speak doubt-filled words, and believe them in our heart, we will receive the negative results that follow.

Proverbs 6:2 tells us, "You are snared by the words of your mouth; you are taken by the words of your mouth." I just don't see where the argument is about this. If we are going to be snared by words, let's be snared by God's Word! Amen! Another verse which goes along with this is Proverbs 18:21, "Death and life are in the power of the tongue, and those who love it will eat its fruit." The words we speak will release either death or life into our circumstances, and we will eat the fruit of those words. This principle is found in the New Testament book of James "And the tongue is a fire, a world of iniquity. The tongue is so set among our members that it defiles the whole body, and sets on fire the course of nature; and it is set on fire by hell." (Jas. 3.6).

The words we speak have the ability to set on fire the course of nature. James is employing this principle in a negative sense by emphasizing it is set on fire by hell, but we can choose to agree with God's Word and use our tongues to set on fire the course of nature in a positive way. When we speak God's Word in faith, life is released affecting the course of nature for our good!

Speak to Your Mountain

I want to point out one more truth from Mark 11:23 before moving on. Just as Jesus spoke to the fig tree, we are told to speak to our mountain. Most people get this backwards. Instead of speaking to the mountain about their God, they speak to God about their mountain! That is not what Jesus said! Of course, the mountain isn't Pikes Peak; the mountain is our problem, the illness, the circumstances we are facing. God has put certain things under our authority and He expects us to do something about it. He is not going to do what He commanded us to do! He expects us to exercise our faith and authority to establish His will and take dominion!

Jesus' teaching continues in Mark 11:24, "Therefore I say to you, whatever things you ask when you pray, believe that you receive them, and you will have them." This verse shows the difference between a human type of faith and the God kind of faith. The natural, human type of faith believes only what can be contacted by the senses. But God's kind of faith believes in things which cannot be seen. The world says, "I'll believe it when I see it. But when it comes to things of God, you are going to believe it before you see it, or you're not going to see it.

Doubting Thomas

A great example of this human type of faith is found in the Apostle Thomas. Jesus appeared to His Apostles after His resurrection;

> Now Thomas, called the Twin, one of the twelve, was not with them when Jesus came. The other disciples therefore said to him, "We have seen the Lord." So he said to them, "Unless I see in His hands the print of the nails, and put my finger into the print of the nails, and put my hand into His side, I will not believe." And after

eight days His disciples were again inside, and Thomas with them. Jesus came, the doors being shut, and stood in the midst, and said, "Peace to you!" Then He said to Thomas, "Reach your finger here, and look at My hands; and reach your hand here, and put it into My side. Do not be unbelieving, but believing." And Thomas answered and said to Him, "My Lord and my God!" Jesus said to him, "Thomas, because you have seen Me, you have believed. Blessed are those who have not seen and yet have believed." (Jn. 20.19-23).

Thomas' faith was based entirely upon physical evidence. He only believed what he could see, not what God said. Thomas had a sense-knowledge type of faith. Many Christians have this kind of faith. They want to receive the blessings and answers to their prayers, but fail to receive because their faith is based only upon what they feel or see. Thomas said, "unless I feel or see, I will not believe." Jesus said, "Blessed are those who have not seen and yet have believed." (v. 29).

In Mark 11:24, Jesus made this God-kind of faith a pre-requisite to receiving answers to prayer. Jesus didn't say we can have anything and everything we ask for. He said we would have what we believe we receive when we pray. We must believe we receive the answer when we pray, not when we see it. The prayer of faith believes it receives and expects it to come to pass when we pray. By faith we must believe God answers our prayers even before we see physical evidence.

Jesus said in Matthew 7:8, "For everyone who asks receives, and he who seeks finds, and to him who knocks it will be opened." If everyone who asks receives, then we know, God always answers! When all of the criteria is met, such as asking in faith, asking according to His will, asking with the right motive and not wavering with doubt, we can be confident that God answers. "Now this is the confidence that we have in Him, that if we ask anything according to His will, He hears us. And if we know that He hears us, whatever we ask, we know that we have the petitions that we have asked of Him." (1 Jn. 5.14-15).

Believe and Receive

A most important aspect of faith to be understood is we are to believe we receive when we pray. As was mentioned previously, Jesus commanded us to believe we receive as a prerequisite to answered prayer. Jesus said in Mark 11:24, "Therefore I say unto you, what things so ever ye desire, when ye pray, believe that ye receive them, and ye shall have them." (KJV). The word "desire" comes from the Greek word *aiteo* (Strong's #154) and simply means "to ask". Jesus was clearly speaking of what we ask for in prayer. The verse illustrates one of the main differences between a God kind of faith and a human kind of faith. A natural, human type of faith believes only what it can contact with the senses, that which we can see, taste, hear, smell, or feel. Often people will say "I'll believe it when I see it." But the God kind of faith believes in things that cannot be seen.

A description of God's type of faith is given in Romans 4:17, "God, who gives life to the dead and calls those things which do not exist as though they did." Another important verse for us to consider is Hebrews 11:1, "Now faith is the substance of things hoped for, the evidence of things not seen." The God kind of faith "sees" things which cannot be seen! In other words, it's not limited by the senses. It believes in that which cannot be seen. Jesus is making this God kind of faith, the faith that believes it receives, and believes that which is not seen, a prerequisite to receiving from God through answered prayer. He said we must believe we receive our answer "when we pray", not when we see the thing we desired. It may take only an instant or it may take longer in the future to manifest, but Jesus said "ye shall have them."

Let's notice another most important statement Jesus made about prayer in Matthew 7:7-8, "Ask, and it will be given to you; seek, and you will find; knock, and it will be opened to you. For everyone who asks receives, and he who seeks finds, and to him who knocks it will be opened." Notice the amazing thing Jesus said, "everyone who asks receives"! This is different than what a lot of people say today. Often we hear people say, "Sometimes the answer is yes, sometimes no, sometimes wait." But where is that at in the Bible? According to Jesus, prayer that meets the requirements outlined in God's word is always answered! You must ask in faith, and ask without wavering. You must ask according to God's will and with the right motives. When the requirements are met, Jesus said everyone who asks receives, God answers! Many times we don't perceive the answer because it comes in the spiritual realm before it is manifested in the natural realm. If we waver from confident faith because we don't instantly see something manifest in the natural realm we can actually abort the manifestation. But God did answer.

Our basic premise must always be based on what God said, not on what we may or may not have received in the past. Truth is only established by what God has told us! By faith we have to believe He is answering our prayers, even if we don't see anything immediately. If we fail to believe, that's doubt. Doubt will cause us not to receive the things we desired. We must resist the temptation to be double-minded. James 1:6-7 says, "But let him ask in faith, with no doubting for he who doubts is like a wave of the sea driven and tossed by the wind. For let not that man suppose that he will receive anything from the Lord; he is a double-minded man, unstable in all his ways."

A good example of God answering prayer and the

answer coming from the spiritual realm is found in the life of the Old Testament prophet Daniel. Daniel, chapter nine, describes a prayer Daniel prayed in an attempt to gain understanding of a prophecy God spoke through Jeremiah the prophet. Jeremiah prophesied that the children of Israel would be in captivity seventy years. They had already been in captivity longer than that. Daniel thought this was a prophecy which hadn't come to pass. So he was praying to gain understanding. The Lord revealed to Daniel it was seventy weeks of years, or four hundred ninety years of captivity. I want to point out the activity associated with Daniel's prayer. Daniel 9:3-4 says,

> Then I set my face toward the Lord God to make request by prayer and supplications, with fasting, sackcloth, and ashes. And I prayed to the Lord my God, and made confession, and said, "O Lord, great and awesome God, who keeps His covenant and mercy with those who love Him, and with those who keep His commandments…

The prayer continues through verse nineteen. Verses twenty through twenty-two describe the manifestation of his answered prayer:

> Now while I was speaking, praying, and confessing my sin and the sin of my people Israel, and presenting my supplication before the Lord my God for the holy mountain of my God, yes, while I was speaking in prayer, the man Gabriel, whom I had seen in the vision at the beginning, being caused to fly swiftly, reached me about the time of the evening offering. And he informed me, and talked with me, and said, "O Daniel, I have now come forth to give you skill to understand. (vv. 20-22).

The angel Gabriel appeared to him while he was still praying!

This is the same angel that appeared to Zacharias to tell him about John the Baptist's conception and to Mary to inform her of Jesus' conception. I can read the whole prayer in less than three minutes. Notice verse twenty-three, "At the beginning of your supplication the command went out and I have come to tell you, for you are greatly beloved; therefore consider the matter, and understand the vision;" The angel manifested and said to him, "At the beginning of your supplications the command went out". As soon as Daniel began to pray God gave a command with the answer! But it took nearly three minutes to manifest. This is an example of a prayer that was prayed and within three minutes the answer was received. As long as it only takes three minutes, most people could believe for three minutes. But, what if it takes three hours, three days or three months? Most people lose their faith if it takes time; because they can't see it or feel it they assume it didn't happen and they say, "I asked and I didn't receive." Often, if the answer doesn't manifest instantly people automatically assume it didn't work because many people are dominated by their senses. The Bible tells us to walk by faith not by sight (2 Cor. 5.7). The average person understands that even in the natural realm there are things happening you cannot see.

As an example, there are sound waves penetrating this room this moment which cannot be seen. Someone may say, "I don't believe there are any radio signals in my room." But all you have to do is plug in a radio and tune in to the signal and listen to the broadcast. In fact, the radio is sometimes referred to as a receiver. In order to access or benefit from the broadcast it must be received. Similarly, God is always on. He isn't on and off. No, His grace is consistent toward us. Ephesians 1:7-8 tells us, "In Him we have redemption through His blood, the forgiveness of sins, according to the riches of His grace which He made to abound toward us in all wisdom and prudence." The riches of His grace are consistently abounding toward us. What we have to do is access His grace by faith. Faith is the receiver which enables us to benefit from His abounding grace! There are many things happening in the spiritual realm which cannot be seen. It is absolutely wrong to assume your prayer isn't working because you can't see it. There's more to it than what we can perceive with our senses or understand with our limited brain.

A great example of this is found in the next chapter. Daniel, chapter ten, records another prayer. One could assume that following the results received in the previous prayer Daniel would have more faith and get better results, instead the opposite occurred, it took longer. Daniel 10:2-3 tells us, "In those days I, Daniel, was mourning three full weeks. I ate no pleasant food, no meat or wine came into my mouth, nor did I anoint myself at all, till three whole weeks were fulfilled." This time he prayed, fasted, didn't anoint himself at all. He was one hundred percent focused on God and it took three weeks to get his answer! Let me be clear. I am using this as an example of the spiritual activity which can take place as a result of our praying. I do not mean to suggest that we should use Daniel's prayer as guidance for our praying. Daniel was an Old Testament man. Jesus had not yet been to the cross. I suggest we learn to pray from New Testament revelation. Amen! Now notice Daniel 10:10-11,

> Suddenly, a hand touched me, which made me tremble on my knees and on the palms of my hands. And he said to me, "O Daniel, man greatly beloved, understand the words that I speak to you, and stand upright, for I have now been sent to you." While he was speaking this word to me, I stood trembling.

The answer manifested three weeks after he prayed. Someone might ask, "Why would God answer one prayer in three minutes and the next in three weeks?" A close examination will reveal God didn't answer one in three minutes and the other in three weeks. Verse twelve tells us, "Then he said to me, "Do not fear Daniel, for from the first day that you set your heart to understand, and to humble yourself before your God, your words were heard; and I have come because of your words." God answered both prayers immediately! Gabriel said his words were heard by God and he was sent by God because of his words.

Never doubt that God hears you! He hears us when we pray and He wants to bless and do good! Both prayers were heard and answered but the manifestation was different. It took three minutes for the first one and three weeks for the second. Remember Matthew 7:8, "For everyone who asks receives…" God answers every prayer based on His Word. He doesn't fail us, but there are things going on in the spirit realm which determine how fast an answer can manifest. If we give up, get depressed and quit before the manifestation we can actually abort that prayer. There could have been tremendous activity in the spirit realm which we can't see or are aware of delaying it. Such was the case in Daniel's instance as is revealed in verse thirteen, "But the prince of the kingdom of Persia withstood me twenty-one days; and behold Michael, one of the chief princes, came to help me, for I had been left alone there with the kings of Persia." The answer was on its way, but the prince of the kingdom of Persia withstood him. Michael had to come and help. There was demonic opposition in the tenth chapter that didn't occur in the ninth. This is something a lot of people fail to understand or factor in. People tend to think if God wanted to do it, He'd just do it.

It's wrong to automatically assume prayer isn't working or didn't get heard or answered because results aren't noticed instantly. In order to be effective we have to believe we receive when we pray and when we speak our faith. We might have to stand for three minutes, three days, or months, but God does not fail us. We partner with Him and He with us as we cooperate with Him in our positive response by faith! Sometimes standing in faith is misunderstood. Standing in faith or standing on the Word does not mean passive patience. To stand in faith means to stand believing and speaking. During the time it takes for an answer to manifest, keep believing the right things. Believe God heard you, believe He answered, believe in what He has already done. Then say the right things. Don't talk the problem, talk about the answer. Your confession should be connected to what God has promised and what God has done not connected to your problem. If you truly believe you receive it, you should be able to thank Him for it, even before you see it!

Jesus Calms a Storm

The story of the wind and waves obeying Jesus is a great example of what I am explaining.

> On the same day, when evening had come, He said to them, "Let us cross over to the other side." Now when they had left the multitude, they took Him along in the boat as He was. And other little boats were also with Him. And a great windstorm arose, and the waves beat into the boat, so that it was already filling. But He was in the stern, asleep on a pillow. And they awoke Him and said to Him, "Teacher, do You not care that we are perishing?" Then He arose and rebuked the wind, and said to the sea, "Peace, be still!" And the wind ceased and there was a great calm. But He said to them, "Why are you so fearful? How is it that you have no faith?" And they feared exceedingly, and said to one another, "Who can this be, that even the wind and the sea obey Him!" (Mk. 4.35-41).

Here is an example of Jesus giving His disciples a clear command, "Let us cross over to the other side." (v. 35).

Jesus was asleep in the boat when a great windstorm arose and the boat was about to sink. "His disciples awoke Him and said to Him, Teacher, do you not care that we are perishing?" (v. 38). This was not a genuine question on their part. It was a criticism and complaint! The disciples were fighting for their lives and Jesus wasn't doing a thing. It's not like He didn't know what was happening. This was a small, open boat filling with water. This wasn't a large vessel which had lower decks Jesus was in, protecting Him from the elements. He had to know about the situation, but He was doing nothing! He wasn't fearful and worried about the circumstance they found themselves in. This brings out an important point. Our faith should be connected to what God has said, not to our circumstance or problem we are facing.

Jesus was able to stay calm in the midst of a storm because of confident assurance! The disciples, on the other hand, wanted Him to do something – bail water, row the boat, adjust the sail, do something! Sometimes we feel like the Lord isn't doing His part. We are fighting to survive, yet it seems like our prayers go unanswered. Where is God? Does He care? The answer is always "yes". God does care, never doubt it. We have to understand Jesus has already done His part. He has defeated the devil; He has won the victory and given us authority. It's not His turn. It's our turn to believe and act on His Word!

Jesus did His part for the disciples when He spoke the words, "Let us cross over to the other side." Jesus is God; anything He says is God's Word and can be acted on. Their part was to believe His Word and put it to work by acting on it by faith. They should have stilled the storm or commanded the boat to stay afloat. Instead, they blamed Jesus. How often do we do the same thing when we feel like the Lord hasn't done His part?

Jesus arose and rebuked the storm, then turned and rebuked

the disciples! "But He said to them, "Why are you so fearful? How is it that you have no faith?" (v. 40). Jesus fully expected them to use their faith to do something about the situation! He expected them to believe what He said and act on it! If you don't think so, then why did He rebuke them? He said they had no faith. Are we to think if Jesus were here with us physically, He would have a different response to our unbelief? No. He expects us to believe and act like it's true! Jesus used His faith to bring God's power and God's will into the crisis situation and He expected His disciples to do the same. He didn't consider their fear and passivity to be okay. Faith does not work through passivity. Battles are not won through inactivity. Faith will take hold of the will of God and stand until God's dominion takes over and the Kingdom is established! There must be some degree of faith present when we pray for miracles. We cannot have the idea, "If God wants it to happen it will happen" or "Whatever will be, will be."

Jairus' Daughter is Healed

Another example is found in Mark chapter five. Jesus had crossed over the Sea of Galilee and came to the area of the region of Gadara where He encountered the demon-possessed man. When the man saw Jesus, he ran and worshiped Him (v. 6). Jesus cast the demons into a large herd of swine which immediately ran over a cliff and drowned in the sea (v. 13). After the deliverance, Jesus crossed over again by boat and came to Capernaum where He found a large crowd awaiting Him.

> And behold, one of the rulers of the synagogue came, Jairus by name. And when he saw Him, he fell at His feet and begged Him earnestly, saying, "My little daughter lies at the point of death. Come and lay Your hands on her, that she may be healed, and she will live. (Mk. 5.22-23).

Awaiting Him in the crowd was a man by the name of Jairus who was a ruler of the synagogue. Jesus had previous experience with Jairus that was not positive. Alfred Edersheim who was a Vienna-born biblical scholar, converted from Judaism to Christianity, writes in his book "Sketches of Jewish Social Life":

> In Capernaum, our Lord's "own city" (Matthew 9:1), there was but one synagogue – that built at the cost of the pious centurion. For, although our Authorized Version renders the commendation of the Jewish elders, "He loveth our nation, and has built us a synagogue" (Luke 7:5), in the original the article is definite: "he hath built us the synagogue. (Edersheim 233).

Edersheim continues:

> As for the ruler of that same synagogue, we know that it was Jairus, whose cry of anguish and of faith brought Jesus to his house to speak the life-giving "Talitha cumi" over the one and only daughter, just bursting into womanhood, who lay dead in that chamber, while the crowd outside and the hired minstrels made shrill, discordant mourning. (Edersheim 235-236).

If Edersheim is indeed correct in his assessment of this, Jesus' prior experience with Jairus was in the synagogue of Capernaum on the Sabbath day recorded in Mark 3:1-2, "And He entered the synagogue again, and a man was there who had a withered hand. So they watched Him closely, whether He would heal him on the Sabbath, so that they might accuse Him." The attitude of the ruler of the synagogue could be paraphrased "If you heal this man in my synagogue on the Sabbath, I'll charge you with blaspheming!" Verse five goes on to tell us, "And when He had looked around at them with anger, being grieved by the hardness of their hearts, He said to the man, "Stretch out your hand." And he stretched it out, and his hand was restored as whole as the other." As a result of his healing, the Pharisees and Herodians plotted how they might destroy Him, apparently at the request of Jairus.

But the next time we're told of Jairus approaching Jesus, it was totally different. Jairus' daughter was dying with no hope of help except for a miraculous intervention which he now believed Jesus could provide! When he saw Jesus at Capernaum's sea shore he humbly fell down at Jesus' feet to beg Him to heal his daughter. Now, he abandoned his legalistic views of religious rule and it didn't matter what day it was or where he was, only that his daughter would live! What happened next is amazing! Mark 5:24 simply says, "So Jesus went with him, and a great multitude followed Him and thronged Him." Jesus showed no anger, vengeance, or retaliation toward the one who had previously attempted to destroy Him! What manner of Man is this? He demonstrated perfectly God's love, forgiveness, and mercy toward the undeserving!

Woman with the Issue of Blood Healed

As Jesus agreed to go with Jairus to heal his daughter, the narrative changes:

> Now a certain woman had a flow of blood for twelve years, and had suffered many things from many physicians. She had spent all that she had and was no better, but rather grew worse. When she heard about Jesus, she came behind Him in the crowd and touched His garment. For she said, "If only I may touch His clothes, I shall be made well." Immediately the fountain of her blood was dried up, and she felt in her body that she was healed of the affliction. And Jesus, immediately knowing in Himself that power had gone out of Him, turned around in the crowd and said, "Who touched My clothes?" But His disciples said to Him, "You see the

multitude thronging You, and You say, 'Who touched Me?'" And He looked around to see her who had done this thing. But the woman, fearing and trembling, knowing what had happened to her, came and fell down before Him and told Him the whole truth. And He said to her, "Daughter, your faith has made you well. Go in peace, and be healed of your affliction." (Mk. 5.25-34).

Verse twenty-seven says, "she heard about Jesus." Here is a woman who sought many physicians and spent her whole livelihood and was not better and had gotten worse, simply because there was no alternative. That is, until she heard about Jesus. This brings out an important law of the Kingdom, "So then faith comes by hearing, and hearing by the word of God." (Rom. 10.17). Faith's point of origin is the Word of God. As we hear the Word, faith comes alive in us. She heard about Jesus and all He had been doing and faith rose in her heart. Hope was ignited and she released this faith statement, "If only I may touch His clothes, I shall be made well." (v. 28). Faith has two parts – believing in the heart and speaking with the mouth. Words are containers that release our faith. Our confession of faith is an important part of receiving from God. She spoke her faith and acted on it.

Luke 8:44 says she, "came from behind and touched the border of His garment". In order to touch the border, she must have been on her hands and knees pressing her way through the crowd to get to Jesus! Faith acts on what it believes! Don't act like it isn't so, act like it is so! According to Levitical law, a woman with an issue of blood was unclean (Lev. 15.19), but also, anyone who touches her was unclean as well. Those who were considered unclean were responsible for warning others of the uncleanness or, to avoid public exposure all together or they could receive harsh treatment if detected. This may explain the fearing and trembling when she spoke to Jesus, or perhaps she was simply trembling under the power of God. Remember that Jesus was standing with Jairus, the one authorized to enforce the punishment prescribed by the Law. When she touched Jesus' garment, power flowed out of Him which stopped the flow of blood and she felt in her body that she was healed.

Many people were pressing Jesus and thronging Him when she touched Him and He turned and said, "Who touched My clothes?" (v. 30). The disciples were shocked and said to Him, "You see the multitude thronging You, and You say, 'Who touched Me?'" (v. 31). Although there were many people touching Him, she was the only one the Bible records being healed. She was the one who placed a demand on His power by faith. She believed she would be healed if she just touched Him! It matters what you believe! Lots of people in the crowd that day probably needed healing, but she was the only one who received it. It's probable everyone had a need of some sort, thus the reason they were pressing Him. If God's willingness to heal determined whether or not healing took place, all of the sick in the crowd would have been healed! This shows us it is not just prayer, or wishing and hoping that saves the sick, rather it is the prayer of faith which saves the sick.

Another important point to note is, Jesus didn't know she was there. He wasn't aware of her presence until God's power flowed out of Him and healed her. I know this is contrary to the way a lot of people think. Most people suppose it was God's mercy and compassion which effected the healing but that's not what Jesus said. He said in verse thirty-four, "Daughter, your faith has made you well." This is illustrating an important truth; healing is governed by spiritual law, not a case by case decision from God based on His feelings toward us! This woman received her healing by the law of faith. Again, I quote Romans 3:27, "Where is boasting then? It is excluded, By what law? Of works? No, but by the law of faith."

This miracle happened because the woman activated the law of faith to appropriate her healing with an attitude that would not be denied, illustrating beautifully the violent taking it by force! We will not advance the Kingdom, or receive miracles through passivity and inactivity, or even passionate pleas and crying. God is compassionate and He is touched by our feelings, but God is not moving in our lives independent of us. He works in us, through us, as we cooperate with Him by faith!

The Healing of Jairus' Daughter *(continued)*

Now the Mark chapter five narrative picks back up with Jairus:

> While He was still speaking, some came from the ruler of the synagogue's house who said, "Your daughter is dead. Why trouble the Teacher any further?" As soon as Jesus heard the word that was spoken, He said to the ruler of the synagogue, "Do not be afraid; only believe." And He permitted no one to follow Him except Peter, James, and John the brother of James. Then He came to the house of the ruler of the synagogue, and saw a tumult and those who wept and wailed loudly. When He came in, He said to them, "Why make this commotion and weep? The child is not dead, but sleeping." And they ridiculed Him. But when He had put them all outside, He took the father and the mother of the child, and those who were with Him, and entered where the child was lying. Then He took the child by the hand, and said to her, "Talitha, cumi," which is translated, "Little girl, I say to you, arise." Immediately the girl arose and walked, for she was twelve years of age. And they were overcome with great amazement. (Mk. 5.35-42).

We're told Jairus received word his daughter had died. As soon as Jesus heard the report spoken to Jairus He said to him, "Do not be afraid; only believe." (v. 36). Jesus needed the positive power of faith working in Jairus, not the negative force of fear. I believe it is important for us to understand in any crisis situation the first report is not the last report! Isaiah 53:1 tells us, "Who has believed our report? And to whom has the arm of the LORD been revealed?" I like to turn this around and say, the arm of the Lord is revealed to those who believe the report of the Lord! In the Bible, the term "arm of the Lord" is a reference to God's redemptive power. God's power is available to those who believe for it!

When Jesus and Jairus arrived at the house He made the comment, "Why make this commotion and weep? The child is not dead, but sleeping." (v. 39). We're told they ridiculed Him. Then He put all of the doubters out of the house. Most of the time people fail to recognize the effect doubt and unbelief have on their faith. Jesus' rejection illustrates this quite well. We're told He went from Capernaum to His own country, Nazareth, with His disciples. Mark 6:2 explains:

> And when the Sabbath had come, He began to teach in the synagogue. And many hearing Him were astonished, saying, "Where did this Man get these things? And what wisdom is this which is given to Him, that such mighty works are performed by His hands!

When they heard Jesus teach they were astonished at His teaching. They began to reason among themselves in verse three, "Is this not the carpenter, the Son of Mary, and brother of James, Joses, Judas, and Simon? And are not His sisters here with us?" So they were offended at Him." They went from astonishment to offense in one verse as they began to doubt Him.

> But Jesus said to them, "A prophet is not without honor except in his own country, among his own relatives, and in his own house." Now He could do no mighty work

there, except that He laid His hands on a few sick people and healed them. And He marveled because of their unbelief. Then He went about the villages in a circuit, teaching. (Mk. 6.4-6).

He could not do mighty works there. It doesn't say He would not, it clearly says, "He could do no mighty work there, except that He laid his hands on a few sick people and healed them." (v. 5). The unbelief of the people in His hometown of Nazareth limited what He was able to do there! We saw examples of what Jesus could do in the previous chapter, including delivering the demoniac, healing a woman of an issue of blood, and raising Jairus' daughter from the dead. But the people's unbelief stopped the flow of the power of God on their behalf. So, "He went about the villages in a circuit, teaching." (v. 6). Sound biblical teaching is the cure for doubt and unbelief.

The Great Commission

Before His ascension to the Father, Jesus commissioned the Church to go forth in His name and power.

> And He said to them, "Go into all the world and preach the gospel to every creature. He who believes and is baptized will be saved; but he who does not believe will be condemned. And these signs will follow those who believe: In My name they will cast out demons; they will speak with new tongues; they will take up serpents; and if they drink anything deadly, it will by no means hurt them; they will lay hands on the sick, and they will recover. (Mk. 16.15-18).

The Lord told us to go heal the sick, cast out devils, and preach the gospel. It is amazing how many people ignore the part of healing the sick and casting out devils and try to establish the Kingdom in word only. Paul the Apostle said,

"For the Kingdom is not in word but in power." (1 Cor. 4.20). The Word needs to be confirmed with signs and wonders following. Jesus didn't commission us to pray for the sick and demon-possessed, but that's the way it is being done in the Church today. Many will say, "Father, we know you can do it." Or, "If it's Your will, please do it." Often we come as beggars asking God to do what He commanded us to do, then we wonder why He didn't heal or deliver. God has already released the healing power for every person on this planet to be healed of every disease! Jesus did it all and then authorized us to go in His name! The early church just took Jesus at His word and began to do it.

A Lame Man Healed

A great example of this is found in Acts 3:1-8:

> Now Peter and John went up together to the temple at the hour of prayer, the ninth hour. And a certain man lame from his mother's womb was carried, whom they laid daily at the gate of the temple which is called Beautiful, to ask alms from those who entered the temple; who, seeing Peter and John about to go into the temple, asked for alms. And fixing his eyes on him, with John, Peter said, "Look at us." So he gave them his attention, expecting to receive something from them. Then Peter said, "Silver and gold I do not have, but what I do have I give you: In the name of Jesus Christ of Nazareth, rise up and walk." And he took him by the right hand and lifted him up, and immediately his feet and ankle bones received strength. So he, leaping up, stood and walked and entered the temple with them— walking, leaping, and praising God.

This man had been lame from his mother's womb. He had been carried daily and laid at the temple gate to beg for alms. Each day he would work the crowd, making eye contact with his arms outstretched in an attempt to attain the greatest benefit from his efforts. Peter and John walked up and heard his request, "Alms for the poor. Alms for the poor". "Then Peter said, 'Silver and gold I do not have, but what I do have I give you: In the name of Jesus Christ of Nazareth, rise up and walk.'" (v. 6). Peter knew he had something to give. He knew he had power and authority. He didn't even pray. He simply used the name of Jesus to release that power. Then he took him by the hand and lifted him up. This was Peter acting on his faith. But it also says the lame man leaped up! This has to be interpreted as faith on his part! He didn't say, "I can't walk! I've been lame all my life!" No, he cooperated by leaping up, then walking, leaping and praising God and went into the Temple with Peter to Solomon's Porch.

The man held on to Peter and John as he began to learn to walk and Peter began to preach his second sermon. He used this miracle to proclaim Jesus and His resurrection. Then he made the tremendous statement in verse sixteen, "And His name, through faith in His name, has made this man strong, whom you see and know. Yes, the faith which comes through Him has given this perfect soundness in the presence of you all."

Peter took responsibility and used the authority given to him in the name of Jesus to heal the man. I believe this is the correct approach. The mindset of the Kingdom ambassador should always be triumphant, victorious, and overcoming. We should be mindful of the Word; the things God has told us to lead us into victory. This is what Jesus meant when He said, "And from the days of John the Baptist until now the Kingdom of heaven suffers violence, and the violent take it by force." (Matt. 11.12). The Kingdom is forcefully advancing and violent men, committed men with a faith that will not be denied, take it by force -- seize it, lay hold of it, and won't let go!

Do We Need More Faith?

Sometimes people believe they don't have enough faith or possibly need extra to accomplish something or to receive from God. There was a time when Jesus' own team felt the same way. It is described for us in Luke 17:1-5:

> Then He said to the disciples, "It is impossible that no offenses should come, but woe to him through whom they do come! It would be better for him if a millstone were hung around his neck, and he were thrown into the sea, than that he should offend one of these little ones. Take heed to yourselves. If your brother sins against you, rebuke him; and if he repents, forgive him. And if he sins against you seven times in a day, and seven times in a day returns to you, saying, 'I repent,' you shall forgive him."

Jesus had been performing miracles, signs, and wonders that had not been done before. His men observed it all, but it wasn't the supernatural power display or the miracles that prompted them to make their request. It was when Jesus spoke to them about forgiving someone seven times in a single day that prompted the response "increase our faith". (v. 5). There is a very important truth to be learned from this. Our faith isn't just for the miraculous. It shouldn't be reserved for use only for the big issues in our lives. No, our faith is for the everyday issues as well. We should use our faith to help us love people and forgive those who have hurt or mistreated us. We should use our faith at home, at work and in our lives to develop and display all of the fruit of the Spirit operating through us. We should use our faith to overcome temptation, habits, and addictions. And to build strong character in our lives. Faith isn't only for the situations we face which seem impossible; it is for the little things as well. This is truly something that will help us to be more victorious in life.

Let's notice Jesus' response to their request to increase their faith. It is in verse six, "So the Lord said, 'If you have faith as a mustard seed, you can say to this mulberry tree, 'Be pulled up by the roots and be planted in the sea', and it would obey you.'" Jesus' response to them was they did not need more faith, they just needed to use the faith they already had. He's saying when a person uses the faith they have it is sufficient. He then continues on to tell the story in verses seven through ten to illustrate this:

> And which of you, having a servant plowing or tending sheep, will say to him when he has come in from the field, 'Come at once and sit down to eat'? But will he not rather say to him, 'Prepare something for my supper, and gird yourself and serve me till I have eaten and drunk, and afterward you will eat and drink'? Does he thank that servant because he did the things that were commanded him? I think not. So likewise you, when you have done all those things which you are commanded, say, 'We are unprofitable servants. We have done what was our duty to do.' (Lk. 17.7-10).

It's not a matter of needing more faith, it is a matter of not using what we have. That's what this story is about. These days this is a little hard for us to relate to because most of us don't have servants working for us. But in Jesus' day it was common for some people to have servants. Most of us would tend to think when a servant has worked hard all day, let him come in and rest and eat. But Jesus' point is if you have a servant, use your servant. This is his job. Then, when you are fed and cared for, he can rest. The point made in response to the apostles' request for more faith was, "You don't need more, just use what you have!" The faith you have is sufficient if you will use it. Faith is our servant, intended to be developed and used.

4 ENDUED WITH KINGDOM POWER

Up to this point I have emphasized the need for Christians to cooperate with God by faith to believe and receive from our Lord; to not settle for less than God's best but to enforce the victory to truly be born again to win. I now want to begin to explore the important role of the Holy Spirit's power operating through the Christian's life and walk of faith.

> The gift of the Holy Spirit, the promise of the Father, was to be bestowed upon the church in the form of a baptism. In the New Testament, this baptism began to be preached by John the Baptist, and his message is recorded in all the gospels and is quoted by Jesus and Peter in the Acts of the Apostles. Matthew and the other writers of the gospels record that Jesus told His disciples: "I indeed baptize you with water unto repentance, but He that cometh after me is mightier than I, whose shoes I am not worthy to bear: He shall baptize you with the Holy Ghost, and with fire." (Matt 3:11 KJV) (Voight 15).

The ministry of the Holy Spirit operating within and through believers is emphasized early in the New Testament even prior to Jesus' ministry through His forerunner, John the

Baptist.

Jesus' Teaching on the Holy Spirit

A number of the teachings Jesus made on the Holy Spirit are recorded by John in his gospel. I want to look at a few of them.

> On the last day, that great day of the feast, Jesus stood and cried out, saying, 'If anyone thirsts, let him come to Me and drink. He who believes in Me, as the Scripture has said, out of his heart will flow rivers of living water.' But this He spoke concerning the Spirit, whom those believing in Him would receive; for the Holy Spirit was not yet given, because Jesus was not yet glorified. (Jn. 7.37-39).

It's possible to read right through these verses and not realize the impact if one does not have some understanding of the details of the Jewish festival called the Feast of Tabernacles. A short discussion will help to grasp the significance of Jesus' comment.

> During the Feast of Tabernacles (Booths or Ingathering), a weeklong celebration for the harvest, the Jews lived in make-shift shelters of branches (booths) to commemorate the Hebrews' journey from Egypt to Canaan, and to thank God for the rich produce of Canaan. The Jews had to take 'choice fruits from the trees, and palm fronds, leafy branches and poplars and rejoice before the Lord your God for seven days'. (Leviticus 23:33-40). In the Temple, 70 bullocks were offered, in sacrifice for the 70 nations of the world. Each day the Law was read, the Temple trumpets sounded a 21-trumpet fanfare and the ritual of "drawing water" was acted out. A priest went with a golden water jug to the Pool of Siloam and solemnly drew out three

"logs" of water. To the accompaniment of the Temple trumpets the water was carried to the top of the altar slope and poured into a silver basin on the western side. Jesus, aware of the spiritual longings of the crowd in the Temple said on the last day of the great festival, "If anyone is thirsty let him come to Me and drink." (John 7:37) (Blackhouse 20).

The Temple would have been filled with possibly tens of thousands of people, on the last day as the festival had risen to a grand conclusion. Just as the Priest pours the water out of the golden jug, Jesus cries out with a loud voice, "If anyone thirsts, let him come to me and drink. He who believes in Me, as the Scripture has said, out of his heart will flow rivers of living water." (Jn. 7.37). Not out of the pitcher, not out of the pool of Siloam, but out of his heart! Jesus publicly proclaimed He was the fulfillment of all the ceremony typified! He was saying, if you are thirsty, drink of Me! John gives the explanation of this in verse thirty-nine: "But this He spake concerning the Spirit, whom those believing in Him would receive; for the Holy Spirit was not yet given, because Jesus was not yet glorified." (Jn. 7.39). John interprets the words of Jesus to refer to the pouring out of the Holy Spirit which was still to come on the Day of Pentecost. Soon the fullness of the Spirit would be a blessing all God's people could experience! John goes on to record the reaction of the people and the authorities in verses forty through fifty-two. The people were excited about this but the chief priests and Pharisees wanted Him arrested!

The Holy Spirit as Our Helper

On the night of Jesus' betrayal and false arrest, He taught the disciples about the Holy Spirit and promised another "Helper" or "Comforter" (KJV): "And I will pray the Father, and He will give you another Helper, that He may abide with you forever— the Spirit of truth, whom the world cannot receive, because it neither sees Him nor knows Him; but you know Him, for He dwells with you and will be in you." (Jn. 14.16-17). And then later in the chapter, "But the Helper, the Holy Spirit, whom the Father will send in My name, He will teach you all things, and bring to your remembrance all things that I said to you." (Jn. 14.26). And, again, two chapters later, "Nevertheless I tell you the truth. It is to your advantage that I go away; for if I do not go away, the Helper will not come to you; but if I depart, I will send Him to you." (Jn. 16.7).

In verse sixteen, Jesus said the Helper would come and abide with us forever. This is important to understand and many Christians don't fully understand this. It is evident by the way many pray. Often we hear well-meaning, but inaccurate prayers asking God to "come be with us" or "go with us as we depart from this place", etc. This is an Old Testament mentality of the Holy Spirit's presence. Under the Old Testament the Holy Spirit came and went among men. David said in Psalm 51:11, "Do not cast me away from Your presence, and do not take Your Holy Spirit from me." He was expressing fear that the presence of the Holy Spirit would depart from him. This is in sharp contrast to Jesus' teaching in the New Testament. Jesus said the Holy Spirit would abide with us forever! He does not come and go from us!

Let me point out that Jesus said in John 14:17, the world cannot receive the Holy Spirit. This means unless a person is born again he or she cannot receive the baptism with the Holy Spirit. Peter used the baptism with the Holy Spirit as proof that the Gentiles had received salvation. Acts chapter eleven records Peter's defense of the Gentiles' new birth. The chapter begins by explaining that the leaders in Judea had heard about Peter's ministry to the Gentiles at Cornelius' house in Caesarea. It says, "those of the circumcision contended with him." (Acts 11.2).

The Jewish leaders argued with Him and were not excited about the Gentiles receiving salvation! Peter then began to recount the story of Cornelius sending for him and the vision he had from the Lord to show that with God there is no partiality between Jew and Gentile. He explained that the Holy Spirit led him to go to the Gentiles, and then said,

> And as I began to speak, the Holy Spirit fell upon them, as upon us at the beginning. Then I remembered the word of the Lord, how He said, 'John indeed baptized with water, but you shall be baptized with the Holy Spirit.' If therefore God gave them the same gift as He gave us when we believed on the Lord Jesus Christ, who was I that I could withstand God? (Acts 11.15-17).

When Peter recounted the story they accepted it as proof that God had granted salvation to the Gentiles! The Gentiles had received the baptism with the Holy Spirit, whom the world cannot receive, proving God was no longer only dealing with Jews!

The Birthday of the Church

Before I can begin to discuss the Promise of the Father, which is the baptism with the Holy Spirit, we must understand that the baptism with the Holy Spirit is not the salvation experience.

> The overarching question that must be addressed at this time is whether the Day of Pentecost is the birthday of the church -- the moment that the disciples were born again in the full sense of the word and received the infusion of the Spirit, or is it a time of the outpouring of the gift of the Holy Spirit upon those who had been born again and received an infusion of the Holy Spirit at an earlier time. (Voight 20).

A most important reference to the Holy Spirit is recorded in the Gospel of John during a post resurrection appearance of Jesus to His disciples:

> When He had said this, He showed them His hands and His side. Then the disciples were glad when they saw the Lord. So Jesus said to them again, 'Peace to you! As the Father has sent Me, I also send you.' And when He had said this, He breathed on them, and said to them, 'Receive the Holy Spirit.' (Jn. 20.20-22).

I have already established that the world cannot receive the Holy Spirit according to Jesus' words from John 14:17. Most people would agree the disciples could not be born again until after Jesus died on the cross as our substitutionary sacrifice and arose as our High Priest to take His blood into the heavenly Holy of Holies to obtain our eternal redemption.

> But Christ came as High Priest of the good things to come, with the greater and more perfect tabernacle not made with hands, that is, not of this creation. Not with the blood of goats and calves, but with His own blood He entered the Most Holy Place once for all, having obtained eternal redemption. (Heb. 9.11-12).

We must answer the question, "Did the disciples receive the new birth when they received the Holy Spirit on the Day of Pentecost, or were they born again at an earlier time?" I believe the disciples were born again at the post resurrection appearance of Jesus when He breathed on them and said to them, "Receive the Holy Spirit" in John 20:22. The Day of Pentecost was not the birthday of the Church, rather it was the day the one hundred twenty believers were endued with the power of the Holy Spirit to live the Christian life. This understanding establishes the fact that the experience of the baptism with the Holy Spirit is subsequent to salvation.

Robert Voight states the position of those who incorrectly view salvation and the baptism with the Holy Spirit as synonymous:

> The persons who believe salvation and the baptism in the Holy Spirit are the same identical experience would say that the disciples were born again on the Day of Pentecost by being baptized in the Holy Spirit. Peter gave the scriptural means for such an experience when he said, "Repent and be baptized every one of you in the name of Jesus Christ for the remission of sins, and ye shall receive the gift of the Holy Ghost." (Acts 2:38). They believe that there is no subsequent experience following salvation and the so-called evidence of speaking in tongues is not a normative experience for all Christians. (Voight 21).

Of course we recognize the work of the Holy Spirit in receiving our salvation. Once we recognize and respond to the love of God, demonstrated to us through Christ, the first thing the Spirit does is produce an inward change. This change allows us to become God's dwelling place on earth and produces relationship. We just can't overemphasize the importance of close, personal, intimate relationship with our Father! So, the Holy Spirit's presence is essential to that relationship. The Bible suggests a dual working of the Spirit of God in those who are Christians. Kenneth E. Hagin agreed:

> The Holy Spirit comes within the believer in the New Birth or as it is sometimes called, conversion, being born again, receiving remission of sins, receiving eternal life, or receiving Christ as Savior and Lord. But on the other side of that dual working, the Holy Spirit comes upon the believer when he or she is baptized in the Holy Ghost that is an experience of the enduement of power. (The Spirit Within...17).

With this premise having been established I will now explore examples from the Scripture of those receiving the mighty Holy Spirit baptism.

Peter in the Garden of Gethsemane

If we take seriously the commission of our Lord to go into all the world and make disciples of the nations, and if we truly desire to win in our personal lives by being the overcomers the Bible describes, we must recognize the need to flow in the supernatural power of God. To be victorious we must have the power of God, the gifts of the Spirit, and signs, wonders, and miracles operating through us to be effective at establishing and advancing the Kingdom of God in our lives. We must not view this as optional! We will not be effective in operating in the supernatural power of God as long as this is viewed as an optional experience! We must be convinced we need it working in us! As long as a person views it as optional, or has the attitude it is okay if it happens and no big deal if it doesn't; if a person isn't convinced this is for them, they will be limited and won't be able to flow consistently in the power of God. Someone may ask, "Are you saying we can't be saved without the baptism with the Holy Spirit?" No, I'm not suggesting that we cannot be saved without the baptism with the Holy Spirit. I would agree one may be saved without it. I am saying, "Why would you want to? Why settle for a powerless life? Why not go ahead and receive all the Lord has provided for us?" Don't stop at the cross, go on to Pentecost and receive this empowering experience!

I believe the transforming ability of this empowering experience is beautifully illustrated in the life of the Apostle Peter. He was powerfully impacted and radically changed by it. I will begin this discussion by examining how it impacted him. We will pick up Peter's story in Matthew 26:31-35:

Then Jesus said to them, "All of you will be made to stumble because of Me this night, for it is written: 'I will strike the Shepherd, and the sheep of the flock will be scattered.' But after I have been raised, I will go before you to Galilee." Peter answered and said to Him, "Even if all are made to stumble because of You, I will never be made to stumble." Jesus said to him, "Assuredly, I say to you that this night, before the rooster crows, you will deny Me three times." Peter said to Him, "Even if I have to die with You, I will not deny You!" And so said all the disciples.

Jesus is predicting Peter's denial. Peter didn't believe it; he even said, "if all are made to stumble because of You, I will never be made to stumble." (v. 33). He then reinforced it with a bold statement in verse thirty-five, "Even if I have to die with You, I will not deny You!" Knowing Peter did deny the Lord shortly after his statement, I believe he sincerely meant it, and he proved it. We can see this from his actions just a short while later in the Garden of Gethsemane which is described for us in John 18:1-11:

When Jesus had spoken these words, He went out with His disciples over the Brook Kidron, where there was a garden, which He and His disciples entered. And Judas, who betrayed Him, also knew the place; for Jesus often met there with His disciples. Then Judas, having received a detachment of troops, and officers from the chief priests and Pharisees, came there with lanterns, torches, and weapons. Jesus therefore, knowing all things that would come upon Him, went forward and said to them, "Whom are you seeking?" They answered Him, "Jesus of Nazareth." Jesus said to them, "I am He." And Judas, who betrayed Him, also stood with them. Now when He said to them, "I am He," they drew back and fell to the ground. Then He asked them again, "Whom are you seeking?" And they said, "Jesus of Nazareth." Jesus answered, "I have told you that I am He. Therefore, if you seek Me, let these go their way," that the saying might be fulfilled which He spoke, "Of those whom You gave Me I have lost none." Then Simon Peter, having a sword, drew it and struck the high priest's servant, and cut off his right ear. The servant's name was Malchus. So Jesus said to Peter, "Put your sword into the sheath. Shall I not drink the cup which My Father has given Me?"

We're told this is an armed detachment of troops there to take Jesus by force. When the soldiers first attempted to take Jesus, Peter pulled a sword and was willing to defend Jesus from a whole detachment of armed soldiers! Peter proved he meant what he said. He swung the sword and severed Malchus' right ear. I suggest he wasn't trying to cut off his ear; he was trying to cut of his head! Malchus ducked and it cut off his ear. We don't have all the detail we would like, but I believe Peter would have continued to fight if Jesus had not stopped him. We're told Jesus said to Peter, "Put your sword into the sheath. Shall I not drink the cup which My Father has given Me?" It's a miracle that Peter didn't die right there at the hands of those soldiers. Peter loved Jesus with all of his heart. He was committed to Him and was willing to give his life to prove it. But he wasn't fully prepared for what he was facing and what he was about to face. There was still a work that needed to be accomplished in him that would take place some fifty days later with the outpouring of the Spirit on Pentecost.

The chapter continues to tell of Peter's denial of the Lord at the courtyard of the high priest. We're told another piece of information which took place after Jesus' death, burial, and resurrection in John 20:19, "Then the same day at evening, being the first day of the week, when the doors were shut where the disciples were assembled for fear of the Jews, Jesus came and stood in the midst, and said to them, 'Peace be with you.'" We see Peter and the others hiding, paralyzed with fear of the Jews. There was still a work to be accomplished in them that would occur in the upper room in Jerusalem on the Day of Pentecost. Peter would be radically changed and would never be the same. Luke recorded Jesus' final words to His disciples prior to His ascension in Luke 24:44-48:

> Then He said to them, "These are the words which I spoke to you while I was still with you, that all things must be fulfilled which were written in the Law of Moses and the Prophets and the Psalms concerning Me." And He opened their understanding, that they might comprehend the Scriptures. Then He said to them, "Thus it is written, and thus it was necessary for the Christ to suffer and to rise from the dead the third day, and that repentance and remission of sins should be preached in His name to all nations, beginning at Jerusalem. And you are witnesses of these things."

Jesus commissioned the Church to go to the nations to preach the gospel in His name. We need to take this seriously; it is the responsibility of us all. It wasn't just the Apostles' responsibility; it is the Church's responsibility! As important as the Commission was and is, Jesus didn't want them to start yet. He said in verse forty-nine, "Behold, I send the Promise of My Father upon you; but tarry in the city of Jerusalem until you are endued with power from on high." This wasn't an optional experience. Jesus didn't view it as optional and neither should we. If it was necessary for them, it is necessary for us as well!

The Promise of the Father

Let's continue now to the Book of Acts record of the events. The Gospel of Luke and the Acts of the Apostles were both authored by Luke. We can clearly see that the Book of Acts picks up where Luke chapter twenty-four left off as is seen in Acts 1:1-4:

> The former account I made, O Theophilus, of all that Jesus began both to do and teach, until the day in which He was taken up, after He through the Holy Spirit had given commandments to the apostles whom He had chosen, to whom He also presented Himself alive after His suffering by many infallible proofs, being seen by them during forty days and speaking of the things pertaining to the kingdom of God. And being assembled together with them, He commanded them not to depart from Jerusalem, but to wait for the Promise of the Father, "which," He said, "you have heard from Me;"

"The former account" is a reference to the third Gospel, which was authored by Luke. Verse four is a direct reference to Luke 24:49, where he used the same terminology, "the Promise of the Father." The term, "Promise of the Father" is the baptism with the Holy Spirit. This is brought out in the next verse, "for John truly baptized with water, but you shall be baptized with the Holy Spirit not many days from now." (Acts 1.5). He said they would receive the Holy Spirit "not many days from now." The outpouring of the Spirit would occur on the Day of Pentecost which was soon to come. After that initial outpouring, the Promise of the Father was a blessing intended to be received and enjoyed by the entire Church. The only time it was ever necessary to wait, or tarry for it was at that particular time because the Promise of the Father had not yet been given. Since then there is no need to wait or spend extended lengths of time seeking Him in an attempt to receive. The baptism with the Holy Spirit is now an experience to be received by faith and is available to all who are born again. I will explain this further later in this chapter as I cover the various examples from the Book of Acts.

Now let's look at a most important verse to be understood, Acts 1:8, "But you shall receive power when the Holy Spirit has come upon you; and you shall be witnesses to me in Jerusalem, and in all Judea and Samaria, and to the end of the earth." Jesus told us what the purpose of the baptism with the Holy Spirit was. The purpose of this experience is to be endued with power for life and service! You shall receive power when the Holy Spirit comes upon you. It is the power from God which enables us to effectively live the Christian life and be productive in advancing the Kingdom of God by proclaiming the gospel. Living the Christian life as intended is not simply a difficult thing to do; it is an impossible thing to do in our own natural strength. God has provided the Holy Spirit's presence and power for us to help us live and forgive and walk by faith to be able to overcome.

In my position as Chaplain at the Kyle Correctional Center I minister to multitudes of men who love the Lord but are held in bondage to addictions to drugs and alcohol. I've listened to their stories of their hatred for the addiction that has cost them so much. Often the cost has been relationships, belongings, and their freedom. They tell of crying out to God for help and forgiveness even as they plunge the needle into their arm; powerless to resist the strong urges compelling them to use. Multitudes of people attempt to live in their own natural strength thinking their own self-control or discipline is sufficient. We are not sufficient on our own. The missing ingredient for many Christian people who love the Lord with all their heart but remain weak, is to receive this empowering of the Holy Spirit! The purpose of the baptism with the Holy Spirit is not speaking in tongues. Speaking in other tongues is a tremendous benefit and provides evidence one has truly received, but should not be viewed as the sole purpose of being Spirit filled. I will explain more about some of the benefits of speaking in tongues in chapter five. The primary purpose of this Promise of the Father is empowerment to be a witness according to Acts 1:8 which is a key verse to a scriptural understanding of this experience.

The Day of Pentecost

In Acts chapter two we find the disciples gathered together in an upper room in Jerusalem just as Jesus had instructed. According to Acts 1:15 there was a group of about one hundred and twenty in all. Acts 2:1-4 describes the glorious scene:

> When the Day of Pentecost had fully come, they were all with one accord in one place. And suddenly there came a sound from heaven, as of a rushing mighty wind, and it filled the whole house where they were sitting. Then there appeared to them divided tongues, as of fire, and one sat upon each of them. And they were all filled with the Holy Spirit and began to speak with other tongues, as the Spirit gave them utterance.

There was a sound of a rushing mighty wind that filled the room. It wasn't a wind; it was the "sound" of a mighty wind. We're also told there were "divided tongues, as of fire". This wasn't a literal fire; this was a manifestation of the glory of God. As God's manifest glory filled the room it must have looked like the room was on fire. It is interesting that John foretold that the Spirit baptism would be by wind and fire in Matthew 3:11-12. Verse four clearly tells us, "And they were all filled with the Holy Spirit and began to speak with other tongues, as the Spirit gave them utterance." As these believers were filled with the Holy Spirit it clearly says they spoke "with other tongues." The phrase "other tongues" refers to spoken languages. The following verses make it clear the crowd of people were made up of different nationalities of people who spoke different languages and dialects. They were able to understand the languages these Galileans were speaking. This was a supernatural utterance given by the Holy Spirit which enabled the Galilean believers to speak in other languages they had never learned. Verses five through seven tell us there were a variety of languages being spoken that day:

> And there were dwelling in Jerusalem Jews, devout men, from every nation under heaven. And when this sound occurred, the multitude came together, and were confused, because everyone heard them speak in his own language. Then they were all amazed and marveled, saying to one another, "Look, are not all these who speak Galileans?" (Acts 2.5-7).

There was a large crowd of international Jews gathered at Jerusalem in observance of the Jewish holiday of Pentecost. Verses eight through eleven continue and inform us of the nationalities represented:

> And how is it that we hear, each in our own language in which we were born? Parthians and Medes and Elamites, those dwelling in Mesopotamia, Judea and Cappadocia, Pontus and Asia, Phrygia and Pamphylia, Egypt and the parts of Libya adjoining Cyrene, visitors from Rome, both Jews and proselytes, Cretans and Arabs—we hear them speaking in our own tongues the wonderful works of God. (Acts 2.8-11).

It is clear these were Jews from other nations who did speak the various languages being spoken, and were confused because the Galileans were able to speak their native languages. In their amazement they began to question what they were experiencing and in an attempt to explain it they simply began to mock and drew the conclusion that they were "full of new wine" (Acts 2.13). In other words, they accused them of being drunk! Probably most Christians can relate to similar experiences. Most of us have tried to explain something we have received from the Lord and received criticism or ridicule from people or often people will dismiss it by attempting to give a natural explanation for a supernatural experience.

Peter's First Sermon

Peter took the lead and stood up before the crowd and began to preach his first sermon! Amazing, when you consider that approximately fifty days prior to this he was paralyzed by fear and even denied the Lord! But now Peter has been changed by this experience of the infilling of the Holy Spirit. He was endued with power which enabled him to boldly stand to preach as we're told in verses fourteen and fifteen, "But Peter, standing up with the eleven, raised his voice and said to them, 'Men of Judea and all who dwell in Jerusalem, let this be known to you, and heed my words. For these are not drunk, as you suppose, since it is *only* the third hour of the day.'" He explained that they were not drunk; it was only nine o'clock in the morning. In the following verses he quoted the Old Testament Prophet Joel claiming this was a fulfillment of his prophecy. Joel prophesied that in the last days God would pour out His Spirit on all flesh accompanied by signs and wonders. Peter's sermon continues in verses twenty-two through twenty-four:

> Men of Israel, hear these words: Jesus of Nazareth, a Man attested by God to you by miracles, wonders, and signs which God did through Him in your midst, as you yourselves also know— Him, being delivered by the determined purpose and foreknowledge of God, you have taken by lawless hands, have crucified, and put to death; whom God raised up, having loosed the pains of death, because it was not possible that He should be held by it. (Acts 2.22-24).

He boldly proclaimed Jesus to the Jewish crowd and made the bold and fearless statement, "you have taken by lawless hands, have crucified, and put to death." (v. 23). Boldness of such a degree that stands in sharp contrast to his previous actions, all as a result of the Spirit's empowering presence in his life. He's no longer a fearful fisherman but has been transformed into a powerful preacher!

As he concludes the sermon he reiterates the bold accusation in verse thirty-six, "Therefore let all the house of Israel know assuredly that God has made this Jesus, whom you crucified, both Lord and Christ." In the following verse we are told they were cut to the heart by his preaching. The conviction must have been tremendous! Their response was "Men and brethren, what shall we do?" (v. 37). My paraphrase would be, "Oh God, what have we done and what are we going to do now?" I will never be able to get over what Peter said next. If it had been me, I know I would have wanted to say, "You dirty dogs. You deserve to die and go to hell for what you have done!" I hope I wouldn't have said it, but I would have wanted to! What Peter said under the inspiration of the Holy Spirit amazes me, "Then Peter said to them repent, and let every one of you be baptized in the name of Jesus Christ for the remission of sins: and you shall receive the gift of the Holy Spirit." (v.38). Amazing! Can you see the grace and mercy of our good God in that statement? Unconditional love extended to men who did not deserve it! If they would repent, God offered to save, forgive and fill them as well with His Spirit.

The next verse is a tremendously important verse to communicate to all; verse thirty-nine begins, "For the promise…". What promise? The Promise of the Father, spoken of in Luke 24:49 and Acts 1:4, the baptism with the Holy Spirit. "For the promise is to you and to your children, and to all who are afar off, as many as the Lord our God will call." (v.39). Peter said the Promise of the Father was for those in the crowd and their children, and even those who are afar off! Who's that? That is us. More than two thousand years later the Promise of the Father is still available, still necessary, still empowering. It wasn't just for the early church, or the disciples. It is available for as many as the Lord our God will call! As a result of Peter's powerful and anointed preaching three thousand souls were added to the Church that day (v. 41). Now, after just one sermon, the Church was three thousand, one hundred and twenty people! The Church was growing as God confirmed His Word with signs and wonders following!

Revival in Samaria

The next major example of believers receiving the Holy Spirit baptism is in Acts chapter eight. As a result of persecution of the Church led by Saul of Tarsus, there was a scattering of the believers. Acts 8:4 says, "Therefore those who were scattered went everywhere preaching the word." This actually turned out to be beneficial because it resulted in the gospel being spread everywhere they went! Philip wound up in Samaria and sparked a tremendous revival!

> Then Philip went down to the city of Samaria and preached Christ to them. And the multitudes with one accord heeded the things spoken by Philip, hearing and seeing the miracles which he did. For unclean spirits, crying with a loud voice, came out of many who were possessed; and many who were paralyzed and lame were healed. And there was great joy in that city. (Acts 8.5-8).

As Philip preached Christ to the Samaritans, multitudes of people received signs, wonders, and miracles. Demons were coming out of people, healings were taking place and it says there was "great joy in that city" (v 8). This is important to note, when the true gospel is preached it is always confirmed with accompanying signs! The story continues by describing Simon the Sorcerer's conversion:

But there was a certain man called Simon, who previously practiced sorcery in the city and astonished the people of Samaria, claiming that he was someone great, to whom they all gave heed, from the least to the greatest, saying, "This man is the great power of God." And they heeded him because he had astonished them with his sorceries for a long time. But when they believed Philip as he preached the things concerning the kingdom of God and the name of Jesus Christ, both men and women were baptized. (Acts 8.9-12).

The people of Samaria heeded Simon the Sorcerer, claiming he was the great power of God because of the supernatural powers operating through him. He flowed in the supernatural but his power wasn't from God; of course it was of the devil. It tells us Simon believed Philip's message of the Kingdom of God and the name of Jesus Christ. Notice that the message the early church preached was the message of the Kingdom; the same message both John the Baptist and Jesus preached! And God confirmed the message with signs, wonders, and miracles!

This caused Simon the Sorcerer to believe which is another important point to note. The supernatural power of God manifesting in the miraculous always caused unbelievers to believe! I believe this is the key to revival. There are many people who plead with God to send revival, like it is all up to Him who experiences revival and who doesn't. This is not the pattern of the book of Acts. Here is an example of a preacher boldly proclaiming the Christ and His Kingdom in power and revival broke out! I don't mean to imply prayer is unnecessary. I believe in prayer, but we cooperate with God by operating in faith and preaching the Word in boldness and power!

Now when the apostles who were at Jerusalem heard that Samaria had received the Word of God, they sent

Peter and John to them, who, when they had come down, prayed for them that they might receive the Holy Spirit. (Acts 8.14-15).

When the news spread to the leaders of the church at Jerusalem they sent Peter and John to help with the revival. We're told when they arrived they prayed for the people to receive the Holy Spirit. "For as yet He had fallen upon none of them. They had only been baptized in the name of the Lord Jesus. Then they laid hands on them, and they received the Holy Spirit." (Acts 8.16-17). Verse sixteen is a significant verse for us to notice. This is one of the clearest examples in the Bible showing that the new birth and the baptism with the Holy Spirit are two separate experiences. We are told they had already been baptized. We know Phillip would not have baptized them unless they were born again! Peter and John laid hands on them and they were then filled with the Holy Spirit clearly illustrating that the baptism with the Holy Spirit is distinct from and subsequent to the new birth. We can also see the early church considered Holy Spirit baptism to be the very next experience to be received from the Lord. It was the normal thing to do!

These were believers who had been baptized in water that Peter and John now laid hands on to receive the baptism with the Holy Spirit. This is the New Testament pattern for receiving the Promise of the Father; the laying on of hands. Verse seventeen clearly tells us, "Then they laid hands on them, and they received the Holy Spirit." These Samaritan believers were now Spirit-filled! But, notice it doesn't say they spoke with tongues. But something did happen, there was a visible manifestation: "And when Simon saw that through the laying on of the apostles' hands the Holy Spirit was given, he offered them money, saying, "Give me this power also, that anyone on whom I lay hands may receive the Holy Spirit." (vv. 18-19).

What did Simon see which caused him to know they had been filled with the Holy Spirit? To be consistent with the other examples in the Book of Acts, we must assume he saw the same thing they saw in Acts chapter two on the Day of Pentecost; they spoke with tongues! It doesn't say they spoke with tongues, but it is implied. I also want to point out when Simon the Sorcerer saw this happen it so impressed him he tried to buy this power! Of course it got him rebuked because you cannot buy the power of God! It's important to note as well that Simon had been observing Philip in the revival. He saw the miraculous signs, wonders and supernatural Kingdom ministry in operation as people were delivered of demonic powers and healed by the power of God and none of that inspired him to try to buy the power! But when he saw men filled with the Holy Spirit he offered them money to get that power! Wow! "But Peter said to him, "Your money perish with you, because you thought that the gift of God could be purchased with money! You have neither part nor portion in this matter, for your heart is not right in the sight of God." (Acts 8.20-21).

Peter said unless he would repent he would have neither "part nor portion in this matter..." The word "matter" comes from the Greek word *logos*. Most of the time in the New Testament *logos* is translated "word". There are four times it is translated "utterance" and in this verse it is translated "matter". (Strong's #3056). It seems Peter is making a reference to the speaking in tongues by saying to Simon, "You will have no part of this matter, this utterance, this speaking in another language as evidence of receiving the baptism with the Holy Spirit! Although this example does not say they spoke with tongues, it is implied.

Saul of Tarsus Converted and Filled with the Holy Spirit

We're told of the conversion of Saul of Tarsus on the road to Damascus in Acts chapter nine. "Then Saul, still breathing threats and murder against the disciples of the Lord, went to the high priest and asked letters from him to the synagogues of Damascus, so that if he found any who were of the Way, whether men or women, he might bring them bound to Jerusalem." (Acts 9.1-2). Authorized by the Jewish leadership, Saul headed toward Damascus for the purpose of further persecuting the Church, literally attempting to destroy her, when he had his experience with the Lord Jesus on the road:

> As he journeyed he came near Damascus, and suddenly a light shone around him from heaven. Then he fell to the ground, and heard a voice saying to him, "Saul, Saul, why are you persecuting Me?" And he said, "Who are You, Lord?" Then the Lord said, "I am Jesus, whom you are persecuting. It is hard for you to kick against the goads." So he, trembling and astonished, said, "Lord, what do You want me to do?" Then the Lord said to him, "Arise and go into the city, and you will be told what you must do." And the men who journeyed with him stood speechless, hearing a voice but seeing no one. Then Saul arose from the ground, and when his eyes were opened he saw no one. But they led him by the hand and brought him into Damascus. And he was three days without sight, and neither ate nor drank. (Acts 9.3-9).

Jesus said to Saul in verse four, "Why are you persecuting Me?" He didn't say, "Why are you persecuting the Church?" Jesus takes it personally when people come against His bride! Then in verse five, Saul responded saying, "Who are you Lord?" Here is a very religious man who thought he was doing the work of God. Can you imagine the guilt, shame and embarrassment which surely came over him now that he realizes this Jesus he has been persecuting is Lord? Jesus' reply to him that he had been kicking against the goads (v. 5) tells us Saul had been under conviction for some time over this. The Greek word translated "goad" is the word *kentron*

(Strong's #2759) and it means "a point, a sting, or goad". This is a reference to an iron instrument with points used to urge on livestock. "It is the same word that is used in Acts 2:37 to describe the conviction of the Holy Ghost on the people who listened to Peter's sermon on the day of Pentecost." (Wommack, "The Acts of the Apostles" 553, footnote 6).

Saul's response to Jesus in verse six was "Lord what do You want me to do?" He was told to continue to Damascus and would then receive further instructions. God then spoke to a disciple in Damascus by the name of Ananias:

> So the Lord said to him, "Arise and go to the street called Straight, and inquire at the house of Judas for one called Saul of Tarsus, for behold, he is praying. And in a vision he has seen a man named Ananias coming in and putting his hand on him, so that he might receive his sight." Then Ananias answered, "Lord, I have heard from many about this man, how much harm he has done to Your saints in Jerusalem. And here he has authority from the chief priests to bind all who call on Your name. "But the Lord said to him, "Go, for he is a chosen vessel of Mine to bear My name before Gentiles, kings, and the children of Israel. For I will show him how many things he must suffer for My name's sake." (Acts 9.11-16).

Saul's reputation had preceded him! Ananias had already been hearing reports of this religious terrorist, but he simply obeyed the Word of the Lord and we are told in verse seventeen, "And Ananias went his way and entered the house; and laying his hands on him he said, "Brother Saul, the Lord Jesus, who appeared to you on the road as you came, has sent me that you may receive your sight and be filled with the Holy Spirit." Up until this time in the Book of Acts the only ones who laid hands on people were the five-fold ministers. But here we have a disciple doing it. This is important to mention; disciples are the ones who should be performing ministry. Ministry isn't reserved for the elite or the super-saints. Disciples should be taught they are capable ministers of the New Covenant authorized to use the name of Jesus in the laying on of hands and ministering to people. Also notice Ananias called him "Brother Saul." This shows us he accepted his conversion. This is significant because he prayed for him to be filled with the Holy Spirit. The experience of the infilling of the Holy Spirit is only for believers. Saul was genuinely converted on the road to Damascus and now has received the baptism with the Holy Spirit through the laying on of hands.

This is the third major example in the book of Acts where a believer received the Promise of the Father, but it doesn't say he spoke with tongues. However, we know Paul did speak with tongues because he wrote about it to the church at Corinth in 1 Corinthians 14:18. He said, "I thank my God I speak with tongues more than you all." So we know Paul was a tongue-talker! We also know the church at Corinth exercised this gift excessively. This was part of his purpose in writing 1 Corinthians; to deal with the problem of abusing the gifts of the Spirit which included tongues and interpretation, and to give them instruction for their use in the order of worship. The church was exercising their gift in abundance. Paul told them he spoke in tongues more than they did! If they had done it decently and in order (v. 40) he would have been commending them rather than correcting them. So, although it does not tell us verbally in Acts chapter nine speaking in tongues accompanied Saul's infilling of the Spirit, it is implied.

Cornelius' Household Filled with the Holy Spirit

Acts chapter ten contains a very important reference to the infilling of the Holy Spirit for us to consider. This is significant because this is where the Gentiles first receive the baptism with the Holy Spirit. God was about to do something awesome through Peter, which is recorded in chapter ten, but He first had to deal with the Jewish mindset in Peter. Acts 9:43 tells us Peter was staying with Simon the tanner, "So it was that he stayed many days in Joppa with Simon, a tanner." It is no coincidence Peter is in Simon the tanner's home. A tanner was considered an "unclean" profession because of the contact with dead animals according to Leviticus 11:39, "And if any animal which you may eat dies, he who touches its carcass shall be unclean until evening." It would seem that even prior to the housetop vision recorded in Acts ten, God was already dealing with Peter about the issue of God's non-partiality. In chapter ten, God would clearly reveal to Peter that no man is considered unclean by God. Pious Jews considered Gentiles to be non-covenant people, unworthy of the things of God. There was an extreme prejudice toward the Gentiles. God dealt with this mindset, then demonstrated that He intended the gospel to go to the Gentiles. Wommack gives this insight:

> Cornelius is only mentioned by name here in Acts 10. However, his conversion is mentioned again in Acts 11:4-17, and referred to in Acts 15:15 and Galatians 2:11-12. The conversion of Cornelius, his kinsmen and friends is one of the most important events recorded in the book of Acts. This is the first recorded account of a Gentile being converted to Christianity (with the possible exception of the Ethiopian eunuch in Acts 8:27-38). Prior to this time the church was made up entirely of Jews or Jewish proselytes who believed that it was impossible for anyone to become a Christian without being circumcised or becoming a Jew first. Through this miraculous set of circumstances, God convinced Peter that the Gentiles were also God's people and candidates for salvation. Although Peter related this incident to the church at Jerusalem, it was still not resolved among all the brethren that the Gentiles could become Christians,

as can be seen in Acts 15:1. At the Jerusalem conference recorded in Acts 15, Paul and Barnabas argued for the conversion of Gentiles without circumcision and the keeping of the law of Moses. James, the head of the Jerusalem church, agreed with Paul and cited the conversion of Cornelius as verification that this was true. It is possible that without Peter having been used to bring the gospel to the Gentiles prior to this, the Jerusalem church and its leaders might have rejected the Gentiles as being heirs with them of salvation. Paul later brought up the instance of Cornelius' conversion to Peter when Peter visited him in Antioch and was reproved by Paul for his hypocrisy. (Gal 2:11-14). (The Acts of the Apostles 559, footnote on Acts 10.1).

In the opening verses of chapter ten we are introduced to Cornelius who was a centurion in the Roman military. A centurion was a noncommissioned Roman military officer responsible for one hundred men. He was seeking God and because he didn't know what else to do, he was praying at three o'clock in the afternoon, the Jewish hour of prayer. He wasn't a Jew, he had no requirement to keep Jewish law or tradition, but because the Jews prayed, he prayed. Verse three tells us, "About the ninth hour of the day he saw clearly in a vision an angel of God coming in and saying to him, 'Cornelius!'" God dealt with this man in a vision. I believe this is important to note; if a man wants to know God and will seek Him, he will find Him! God will reveal Himself to anyone who will seek Him. Verse four continues, "And when he observed him, he was afraid, and said, 'What is it Lord?' So he said to him, 'Your prayers and your alms have come up for a memorial before God." In a vision Cornelius saw an angel who brought him instructions from God. Cornelius' first response was fear. I don't think this is because an angel is such a frightening being, I think it is more likely that the fear resulted from the supernatural occurrence. Most people aren't accustomed to seeing an angel in a vision as a common experience, so there was a moment of fear. The angel then instructed him to send men to Joppa to find Peter at Simon the tanner's house. Cornelius then sent two servants and a soldier to find Peter.

The next day Peter was up on the roof top about noontime praying. Verses ten and eleven tell us, "Then he became very hungry and wanted to eat, but while they made ready, he fell into a trance and saw heaven opened and an object like a great sheet bound at the four corners, descending to him and let down to the earth." In the vision the sheet contained animals which the law declared unclean. This vision was repeated three times. Each time there was a heavenly voice insisting he eat them in violation of his Jewish convictions. Peter argued with the Lord; "And a voice spoke to him again the second time, 'What God has cleansed you must not call common.'" (v. 15).

This vision was illustrating to Peter that the Gentiles were no longer considered unclean. God revealed to Peter He is no respecter of persons and there is no partiality with Him. Just as Peter was dwelling upon and meditating the meaning of this, there was a knock on the door. Cornelius' men had found him. "While Peter thought about the vision, the Spirit said to him, 'Behold three men are seeking you. Arise therefore, go down and go with them, doubting nothing, for I have sent them.'" (vv.19-20). Peter went downstairs to meet them and we are told in verse twenty-three, "Then he invited them in and lodged them. On the next day Peter went away with them and some brethren from Joppa accompanied him." Peter probably would not have been willing to go with them to Cornelius' home if God had not spoken to him so clearly. Notice how much Peter's attitude had changed; he stayed in the home of a tanner, he invited Gentiles into the home to stay with him, and then went with the Gentiles to Cornelius' house. God had clearly accomplished a work in Peter's life that enabled him to be used by God in a way that could not have happened prior.

After arriving at Cornelius' house they found that in his anticipation of Peter's arrival, Cornelius had gathered a crowd of his family and friends. As Peter walked in Cornelius fell at his feet to worship him (v. 25)! Clearly Cornelius was confused! Peter stopped him from worshiping a man, as a man of God should do. After a few moments of Peter and Cornelius explaining their experiences with God to each other concerning God's dealings with each man, Peter began to preach to those of Cornelius' house. In the sermon Peter gave a brief but descriptive summary of the life and ministry of Jesus and "while Peter was still speaking these words, the Holy Spirit fell upon all those who heard the word." (v. 44). It happened just as it had happened on the Day of Pentecost. Peter was still preaching, he had not yet stopped to lay hands on them, and they were all filled with the Holy Spirit.

Verse forty-six clearly says, "For they heard them speak with tongues and magnify God." The Jewish Christians who were present knew the Gentiles had received the gift of the Holy Spirit because they heard them speak with other tongues. This makes it clear to us speaking in tongues is at least one initial evidence of being filled with the Holy Spirit. The text records Peter's response to this, "Can anyone forbid water, that these should not be baptized who have received the Holy Spirit just as we have? And he commanded them to be baptized in the name of the Lord. Then they asked him to stay a few days." (vv. 47-48). It was immediately made clear to Peter that these were genuine converts to Christianity, having now been filled with the Holy Spirit, so he then proceeded to have them baptized with water.

Twelve Disciples Receive the Holy Spirit in Ephesus

The latter part of the Apostle Paul's second missionary journey brought him to Ephesus. Acts 18:19 relates that soon after his arrival he made his way to the local synagogue to share the gospel with the Jewish community there. Although they requested he stay with them longer (v. 20), this visit was cut short because he had taken a vow in Cenchrea. This vow is difficult to specify because Scripture doesn't give the specific details. If one is to assume this was a Nazarite vow, there would have been certain rituals which must be fulfilled. Rick Renner describes the events which would have followed a Nazarite vow:

> This ceremonial vow to abstain from strong drink and from cutting one's hair had great moral and religious significance to the Jews; therefore, some scholars believe that Paul may have made this vow to commend himself to the Jews for the purpose of winning some to Christ (see I Corinthians 9:20).

> According to Jewish law, once a Nazarite vow was made, only 30 days were allowed for the fulfillment of all the rituals connected to the vow, and a portion of those rituals could only be fulfilled at the temple in Jerusalem. This meant that Paul had to leave Ephesus and arrive at Jerusalem before the 30 days were completed. (Renner 201).

This would explain why the Apostle's visit was short. Apparently he was able, in the short time, to impact the Jews by sowing seeds of the gospel because they requested he stay longer so they could learn more. When he departed he left Priscilla and Aquila behind to continue the work in his absence. They must have been able to continue to minister to the Jews who were interested in the synagogue week after week until one time they met a man by the name of Apollos. We aren't given many details about their encounter with him, but it would seem they were impressed by hearing his lectures and had the opportunity to take him aside to explain the gospel to him more clearly. Being disciples of Paul they would have had significant understanding of Pauline revelation which was unknown to Apollos. Acts 18:24-26 gives us some insight into this man:

> Now a certain Jew named Apollos, born at Alexandria, an eloquent man and mighty in the Scriptures, came to Ephesus. This man had been instructed in the way of the Lord; and being fervent in spirit, he spoke and taught accurately the things of the Lord, though he knew only the baptism of John. So he began to speak boldly in the synagogue. When Aquila and Priscilla heard him, they took him aside and explained to him the way of God more accurately. (Acts 18.24-26).

From these few verses we learn Apollos was "an eloquent man and mighty in the Scriptures" (v. 24); apparently a learned man with a unique speaking ability. Verse twenty-five lets us know he was "fervent in spirit, he taught accurately the things of the Lord, though he knew only the baptism of John". When the Apostle Paul returned to Ephesus he found twelve men who the Bible calls disciples who had not heard of the Holy Spirit. It is uncertain how much time elapsed between the events related in Acts 18:24-28 but apparently it was enough that Apollos was able to emerge as a leader in the church at Ephesus. It would seem he had influence among some of the believers prior to Aquila and Priscilla enlightening him. (v. 26).

Wommack has this to share:

> Apollos was a Jew, born at Alexandria in Egypt. Special mention is made of Apollos' powerful ability to communicate and his knowledge of the Scriptures; therefore, they must have been very impressive.

> Apollos knew only the baptism of John the Baptist. This would imply that he received his revelation of the

Messiah from John the Baptist, but somehow missed the ministry of Jesus Himself, or if exposed to the ministry of Jesus, he left before the establishment of the Church on the Day of Pentecost. It is possible since Apollos was from Alexandria, that Apollos was in Jerusalem for one of the feasts when he heard the message and believed, then went back home, thus missing the complete gospel.

Regardless, it is clear that Apollos was preaching that Jesus was the Christ. The thing that was missing was that he was not aware of the ministry of the Holy Spirit. This can be seen by the disciples that Paul encountered on his third missionary journey in Ephesus. These twelve men were believers in Jesus, but they had never heard of the Holy Ghost. When Paul asked these unto what they were baptized, they answered, "unto John's baptism" (Acts 19:3). This no doubt reflects that they were converts of Apollos during his ministry in Ephesus before Aquilla and Priscilla instructed him." (Acts of the Apostles 608, footnote 1).

Paul's third missionary journey brought his return to Ephesus. We're told in Acts 19:1-2:

And it happened, while Apollos was at Corinth, that Paul, having passed through the upper regions, came to Ephesus. And finding some disciples, he said to them, "Did you receive the Holy Spirit when you believed?" So they said to him, "We have not so much as heard whether there is a Holy Spirit.

It would seem these disciples were in the same spiritual state Apollos was in prior to his encounter with Priscilla and Aquila. As Paul spoke with them, he discovered that their experience was incomplete. They had not heard of the Holy Spirit! His next question to them was, "Into what then were you baptized?" So they said, "Into John's baptism." (verse 3).

These were men who had been born again by hearing that Jesus had come to die for their sins, but they had not been baptized with the Holy Spirit! Paul was amazed they had been born again without hearing about the Holy Spirit baptism. This makes it clear that Paul included the message of the baptism with the Holy Spirit as part of the gospel message he shared. This is clear Bible evidence that it should be part of the message we share! Often, I find believers in this very same spiritual state. They are genuinely born again, but have not heard of the Promise of the Father. The Spirit-filled life should not be odd or unusual Christianity. It should be normal Christianity. The next experience for the one who puts faith in Jesus as Savior and Lord should be to put faith in Jesus to receive the mighty baptism of the Holy Spirit!

Ephesus was a city with a large population at the time, so it is possible these men simply never had the opportunity to hear Aquila and Priscilla minister. It is likely, just as Apollos, they had heard of Jesus and the mighty works He had done but had not received the complete gospel message. Acts 19:4-5 relates: "Then Paul said, 'John indeed baptized with a baptism of repentance, saying to the people that they should believe on Him who would come after him, that is, on Christ Jesus.' When they heard this, they were baptized in the name of the Lord Jesus." Paul corrected their spiritual condition by re-baptizing them and then "when Paul laid hands on them, the Holy Spirit came upon them, and they spoke with tongues and prophesied." (v. 6).

The Holy Spirit was received through the laying on of hands and it clearly says they spoke in tongues and prophesied. Again we see in this instance, speaking with tongues is emphasized as the initial evidence they had genuinely been filled. Once these men were born again there was no need for them to wait to be filled with the Holy Spirit. This should solidify for us that this is the New Testament pattern. Paul recognized the importance of leading those men into the fullness of complete salvation and made sure he didn't leave them until it was completed.

My Experience of Receiving the Promise of the Father

My experience is similar to the twelve disciples of Acts nineteen in that many years of my life passed before I had knowledge of the Promise of the Father. There's never been a time in my life that I didn't know about Jesus. My mother taught me about the Lord from an early age. She took me to church and encouraged me to have a relationship with the Lord, but as I grew older, unfortunately my relationship with God wasn't a priority in my life. As a result, I knew little about God and Jesus and nothing about the Bible. I have only myself to blame because the opportunity was there, I just didn't take advantage of it. I was baptized as a teenager but honestly, I didn't grow spiritually at all. I may have been saved, but there was little fruit to show it.

I consider my relationship with the Lord to have begun in 1981. I was working on a construction job in Dinosaur, Colorado. We were building a railroad grade from Rangely, Colorado to Vernal, Utah. I was a laborer on the job and one of the foremen was a man by the name of Darrell Dunn. I had worked with Darrell on a previous construction job developing a mine site in the oil shale of Parachute, Colorado. Darrell was a strong believer and had been witnessing to me since the first job together in Parachute. When that job ended, it was actually Darrell who helped me get the next position in Dinosaur. Darrell continued to witness to me and God was using him to minister to my life. As I look back on it, I believe there was a spiritual battle for my life. The company I worked for was from Utah and employed many Mormons, including a man who was the foreman of my crew. We became friends and he was sharing his spiritual persuasion with me as well!

It was during the winter of 1981 that I made my decision to commit my life to the Lord. Darrell had been witnessing to me for about one and a half years. It may have looked like it wasn't working, but it was! God was drawing me by His Spirit. I was going through some very difficult financial times and as fall arrived there were times we were unable to work due to weather conditions. I couldn't afford to miss work and one day, sitting at home, I picked up a large family Bible I had won at a church revival as a teenager. Because I never read the Bible, I knew nothing about it. I didn't even know John 3:16. I opened that family Bible to the front and found an index of "Select Scriptures for Special Needs". As I scanned the page, I found the heading "When Worry Overcomes". I was worrying about finances. It listed Matthew 6:19-34. I located the passage and began to read Jesus' words and for the first time in my life I was being ministered to by God's Word! It was awesome! It stirred the desire for more in me and I began to talk to my friend Darrell about it. He invited me to his home for dinner and Bible study. It was that very night, driving home from his place, when I made the choice to serve Jesus! Praise God!

We began months of weekly Bible study together as he discipled me one on one. It was a tremendous time of spiritual growth and development which changed my life forever. Darrell strongly believed the message of the Word of Faith to include the baptism with the Holy Spirit and speaking in other tongues. As he taught me, I believed and not long after, allowed him to pray with me to receive the experience. Unfortunately, my understanding was extremely limited, especially where receiving by faith was concerned. I didn't know how to cooperate with God and receive by faith, therefore I was hindered in receiving. As time passed, the job ended and I returned to my home on the eastern slope of Colorado in Canon City. By that time, I loved the Lord dearly, had grown much spiritually and was eager to get involved in a good church. After visiting several, I found a

Foursquare Church in town and began to fellowship with them. They preached the baptism with the Holy Spirit and divine healing. There was a good worship ministry and I continued to seek the Lord. Over the course of the next year I was prayed for several times to receive the Promise of the Father. Each time I came away frustrated and discouraged because I wasn't receiving from the Lord.

Time passed and one day an evangelist was at our church and scheduled to preach on a Sunday night. He preached on the baptism with the Holy Spirit in the evening service. At the end of the sermon he gave an altar call for anyone wanting to receive. I went forward with six others. We lined up at the altar area – three on my right and three on my left. The evangelist began on my right by laying hands on the first person in line and prayed for them to receive. The person fell under the power speaking in tongues! He just touched the next two beside me and they fell, speaking in tongues! It was exciting! He came to me, laid his hands on my head and began to pray. Nothing! I didn't fall. I didn't shake. I didn't speak in tongues. He continued to minister to me for a few moments then I uttered a few sounds. He excitedly said, "That's it! You got it!", and proceeded to minister down the line to my left. Each time he touched their heads, they fell to the floor speaking in tongues. The next thing I knew they dismissed the service and the pastor's wife rushed up to me, because she knew I had been seeking. She said, "Praise God, Brother Mike, you got it!" I said, "I did? I'll be honest, I'm a little disappointed. I didn't know it was going to be like this."

You see, I didn't have anyone who could explain it to me clearly as I've attempted to do in this chapter. I had the misconception that the Spirit of God would come on me and take control and it would be all Him and none of me. I would just stand there with eyes closed, mouth open, tongue out, as if to say, "Do it Lord, take me. Make me speak in tongues." I was very concerned, and determined to be genuine. I believed, but refused to fake anything. It would be all God or nothing at all! And that's what I was getting – nothing at all. I thought in God's sovereignty He'd do it all. I didn't understand that the Holy Spirit does not speak in tongues! He gives the utterance but it is our voice, our mouth, and our tongue making the sounds. We do have to receive by faith and cooperate with the Holy Spirit to receive.

When I minister this to people I always point out Acts 2:4, "And they were all filled with the Holy Spirit and began to speak with other tongues, as the Spirit gave them utterance." Who spoke in tongues? They did. What did the Spirit do? He gave the utterance. The Holy Spirit doesn't often communicate with us mouth to ear. He can. There are scriptural examples of people hearing an audible voice, but mostly, God communicates with us Spirit to spirit. "God is Spirit, and those who worship Him must worship in spirit and truth." (Jn 4.24). It's important to understand that the utterance will come to your spirit, then process through your soul so you can speak it out your mouth. He doesn't speak in tongues. He gives the utterance then we choose, as an act of our will, to articulate the utterance with our mouth, voice, and tongue. So with this understanding, I ask people to whom I minister, "Will you speak in tongues? If you will, then you will. If you won't then you won't."

This devotional language isn't being formulated in the mind. 1 Corinthians 14:14 says, "For if I pray in a tongue, my spirit prays, but my understanding is unfruitful." As the utterance processes through the soul, the will is involved but the understanding is unfruitful. The soul is three parts, mind, will, and emotions. The utterance bypasses the mind but it does not bypass the will. This is why the understanding is unfruitful. It is a language we do not understand with the mind.

Well, back to the Sunday evening service when I

received. The pastor's wife was excited for me, but I was discouraged because it didn't happen as I thought it would. She simply said, "Can I pray for you?" She reached up, laid her hand on my head and prayed a simple prayer, "Father, I pray that this gift will manifest itself like rivers of flowing water. In Jesus' name. Amen." I went home and went to bed since I had to go to work the next morning. Several times that night I awoke, fluently speaking in tongues in my heart. And I've fluently spoken in tongues any time I choose to since then! Thank you Jesus!

It's important to understand this is a gift given by God for our benefit. It isn't just a one-time good deal which happens when we receive the Promise of the Father then never to be used again. Use it often! The more you exercise the gift the more fluent it becomes and the more normal it will seem. It will always be supernatural but it will become the "normal" experience for us!

Michael R. McComb

5 BENEFITS OF SPEAKING WITH OTHER TONGUES

I have covered the five major examples in the Book of Acts of believers receiving the baptism with the Holy Spirit. I've pointed out the initial evidence of the infilling of the Spirit is when one is given the ability to speak in other tongues. An important question you may ask is, "How can I know I have been filled with the Holy Spirit?" Certainly, there should be many evidences in life's experience which would indicate a life empowered by the Holy Spirit. I appreciate Menzies and Horton's thoughts on this subject:

> However, the real question is not the long range result of the baptism in the Spirit, but the immediate indication that one may point to as a witness of the experience itself. Has God provided such an indicator? If one concludes that the Book of Acts is not only a descriptive history, but also has a theological purpose, and that the experience of the Apostolic Church, which it records, is normative for the Church of all ages, then one can answer the question with a resounding yes. (Menzies and Horton 135).

When a person confesses Jesus as Lord and is born again there is no outward manifestation of the new birth. A person may exhibit tremendous joy, even dance around or shout, but those things are not evidence of salvation. The Bible tells us the only thing we need to do to be born again is to believe in our hearts that God raised Jesus from the dead and confess with our mouth that He is Lord and Savior (Rom. 10.9-10). When we do that with genuine faith we are born again. No outward manifestation is necessary. We simply believe and receive it by faith! However, as I have pointed out in the previous chapter when the Holy Spirit comes upon us there is a manifestation. In Acts, chapter two, one hundred-twenty believers received the initial outpouring of the Holy Spirit and Acts 2:4 clearly says, "And they were all filled with the Holy Spirit and began to speak with other tongues, as the Spirit gave them utterance."

As I stated in chapter four, Acts chapter nineteen describes the Apostle Paul's travels to Ephesus where he found twelve men who were already born again. We know they were born again because the Bible calls them disciples in Acts 19:1-2,

> And it happened, while Apollos was at Corinth, that Paul, having passed through the upper regions, came to Ephesus. And finding some disciples he said to them, "Did you receive the Holy Spirit when you believed?" So they said to him, "We have not so much as heard whether there is a Holy Spirit.

These were not the Pharisee's disciples or someone else's disciples. They were disciples of the Lord Jesus resulting from Apollos' ministry. It is apparent to me that Paul believed the normal experience for anyone who was born again was to proceed on and receive the baptism with the Holy Spirit! These men had been told about salvation through faith in Jesus but had not been told about the Holy

Spirit. Verse six tells us, "and when Paul had laid hands on them, the Holy Spirit came upon them, and they spoke with tongues and prophesied." It clearly tells us there was a manifestation that occurred when they received the Holy Spirit. One of the most significant examples of this is when the Gentile converts, Cornelius, his kinsmen, and friends received the Holy Spirit. As noted previously, Acts chapter ten records one of the most important events in the Book of Acts. After having been dealt with by God concerning his Jewish mindset, Peter learned that there is no partiality with God. He agreed to go to Cornelius' house where he preached the gospel to the Gentiles who had gathered. We're told in Acts 10:44-46:

> While Peter was still speaking these words, the Holy Spirit fell upon all those who heard the word. And those of the circumcision who believed were astonished, as many as came with Peter, because the gift of the Holy Spirit had been poured out on the Gentiles also. For they heard them speak with tongues and magnify God.

There was an outward manifestation of speaking with tongues when they received. What makes this so significant is revealed in the next chapter. When the Apostles and brethren of the Jerusalem church heard that the Gentiles had received the word of God, they were not excited about it! When they saw Peter they actually began to argue with him, "And when Peter came up to Jerusalem, those of the circumcision contended with him." (Acts 11.2). Peter then began to recount the whole story to them. When he got to the part of the Gentiles receiving the Holy Spirit, it ended the argument!

> And as I began to speak, the Holy Spirit fell upon them, as upon us at the beginning. Then I remembered the word of the Lord, how He said, 'John indeed baptized with water, but you shall be baptized with the Holy

Spirit.' If therefore God gave them the same gift as He gave us when we believed on the Lord Jesus Christ, who was I that I could withstand God?" When they heard these things they became silent; and they glorified God, saying, "Then God has also granted to the Gentiles repentance to life." (Acts 11.15-18).

The Jewish leadership accepted it as proof that God had granted salvation to the Gentiles. Now they knew for certain God was not only dealing with the Jews! The baptism with the Holy Spirit with the evidence of speaking with other tongues was convincing proof of the Gentiles' genuine conversion. Proof positive because Jesus had told them in John 14:16-17,

> And I will pray the Father, and He will give you another Helper, that He may abide with you forever— the Spirit of truth, whom the world cannot receive, because it neither sees Him nor knows Him; but you know Him, for He dwells with you and will be in you.

One must be born again to receive the Holy Spirit, clearly exemplifying that the baptism with the Holy Spirit is subsequent to the new birth.

Speaking in tongues is important for many reasons, certainly more than to prove you have received the Holy Spirit. It should not simply be a one-time experience; it should be part of everyday life. It is a way to communicate directly from our heart to the Father, bypassing the limitations posed by our human brain with its doubts and fears. It builds us up on our most holy faith and releases the hidden wisdom of God. Although this will not be an exhaustive exposition on the subject, I do want to expound on some of the most important reasons we should speak in tongues to help understand the relevance to our daily lives and relationship with our Father as well as its significant help in empowering us to live victoriously!

Tongues and the Corinthian Church

I will begin by examining a few verses from 1 Corinthians chapter fourteen. But first, it will help to understand something about Paul's purpose and intent in writing this important book. Paul makes it clear from the beginning of the first epistle to the Corinthians that his main purpose in writing this letter was to correct the carnality which had damaged the unity of the believers. He says in chapter one verse ten: "Now I plead with you, brethren, by the name of our Lord Jesus Christ, that you all speak the same thing, and that there be no divisions among you, but that you be perfectly joined together in the same mind and in the same judgment."

Paul dealt with the disunity in three main areas. First, a difference of opinion among the people of who they should be following. Some claimed Paul as their spiritual leader, some Apollos, and some Peter. Second, he reprimanded the believers for their immoral conduct. And thirdly, he dealt with the conduct of the Corinthians in their church services: specifically, their practices concerning the observance of the Lord's Supper in chapter eleven, and then in the operation of the gifts in the Church in chapters twelve through fourteen. The Corinthian church was a Spirit-filled church with all of the gifts in manifestation. But there was an abuse of the gifts, so Paul wrote to give instructions concerning their operation. There is much we can learn about the use of speaking in tongues from his instruction. As I have mentioned, it is important for believers to speak in tongues often, not just at church! Speaking in tongues should be a part of life. Our problems aren't at church; our problems are in life. It is a tool at our disposal to help us in life!

I would first like to point out 1 Corinthians 14:2, "For he

who speaks in a tongue does not speak to men but to God, for no one understands him; however, in the Spirit he speaks mysteries." This clearly teaches us when we speak in tongues we speak to God, not to men! Speaking in tongues is not for the purpose of communicating with men, but is for the purpose of communicating with God!

> Many people question what is accomplished by speaking in tongues. There are four verses in this chapter where Paul gives us insight on this. In this verse, Paul says we are speaking mysteries. In verse four Paul says we edify our self through speaking in tongues. Verse fourteen says our spirit is the part of us that prays in tongues, and verse seventeen says we are giving thanks unto God when we speak in tongues. (Wommack, "1 & 2 Corinthians" 943, footnote 4).

When we speak in tongues we are speaking mysteries to God. Paul said in verse thirteen those who speak in tongues should pray for the interpretation. When we pray in tongues our spirit is praying through the power of the Holy Spirit. Normally our understanding is unfruitful because the utterance isn't originating in our mind. But we can pray for interpretation so our understanding can become fruitful. When done correctly, speaking in tongues and receiving the interpretation can benefit us greatly by opening the door to revelation knowledge from the Holy Spirit! What a tremendous tool God has given us to help us gain depth of understanding!

We Edify Ourselves

Next, notice 1 Corinthians 14:4, "He who speaks in a tongue edifies himself, but he who prophesies edifies the church." When we speak in tongues we edify ourselves! The word "edifies" comes from the Greek word *oikodomeo* and is defined by Strong's Exhaustive Concordance as "to be a house-builder, construct, confirm, build, builder, building, build up, edify, or embolden." (Strong's #3618). The reference to a building is why a house came to be known as an edifice. The application in this case is to be "built up". We must know when we pray in tongues we edify ourselves or build ourselves up! Praying in tongues lifts us up in the spirit. What an awesome tool we have been given from God to use to lift ourselves up from depression and discouragement. The world's answer for depression or moodiness is to turn to medication. I have a better answer – start praying in the spirit to build yourself up, to charge yourself as one would charge a battery. Praying in tongues will lift our focus out of the fleshly realm and help us to be more spiritually-minded where there is life and peace. Romans 8:5-6 tells us: "For those who live according to the flesh set their minds on the things of the flesh, but those who live according to the Spirit, the things of the Spirit. For to be carnally minded is death, but to be spiritually minded is life and peace."

Carnal-mindedness is constantly dwelling on the things of the flesh, which tends to produce death, or those things which tend toward death, such as anger, frustration, discouragement, etc. But spiritual mindedness is dwelling on the things of the Spirit which produces life and peace. Someone has said, "I don't want to be so heavenly minded that I'm no earthly good!" Don't worry about that! The ones who have done this world the most good are the heavenly minded ones! Amen! You are supposed to be spiritually minded and praying in the spirit will help you do so. This God-given ability to edify ourselves is tremendous! Too many Christians depend on others to build them up. Often, I find people who are satisfied with someone else's revelation or worship. They come to church with the attitude, "Just feed me Pastor!" and are like baby birds in the nest with their mouths open hoping to be nourished. Rather than actively participating in the worship service they sit back, satisfied to let others or the worship leader do the worship. We are thankful for pastors and teachers who are gifted and have strong revelation to help us grow and understand, but this should not replace our own motivation to build ourselves up. If there were no other benefit to be derived from this gift, this would be reason enough to want to pursue it. Another New Testament scripture which supports this thought is Jude 1:20, "But you, beloved, building yourselves up on your most holy faith, praying in the Holy Spirit," A vital part of our spiritual growth is praying in the Holy Spirit. We are built up on our most holy faith when we do so. Pastor Bob Yandian agrees in his comments about this verse in Jude 20 and 1 Corinthians 14:4:

> The Greek word in both these verses is oikodomeo which means "to build up" as in the building of a house (oikios means "house" and kodomeo means "to build"). In the ancient world, they build structures one brick at a time, in a similar way, speaking in tongues will build and strengthen your faith day by day. (Fellowshipping with God 24).

A Rest and Refreshing

Paul brings out another aspect of edifying ourselves with his reference to Isaiah 28:11-12. In 1 Corinthians 14:21 he quotes the Isaiah passage, "In the law it is written 'with men of other tongues and other lips I will speak to this people; And yet, for all that, they will not hear Me' says the Lord." By including Isaiah's prophetic reference to the gift of speaking in other tongues, Paul claims its fulfillment in the Church age. Isaiah 28:11-12 tells us,

> For with stammering lips and another tongue He will speak to this people, To whom He said, "This is the rest with which You may cause the weary to rest," And, "This is the refreshing"; Yet they would not hear.

Remember, the outpouring of the Holy Spirit with the evidence of speaking in other tongues did not occur until the Day of Pentecost recorded in Acts chapter two, some seven hundred to eight hundred years after Isaiah's life and prophecy. When the Holy Spirit inspired Isaiah to pen this prophecy he had never heard anyone speak in tongues! The Holy Spirit was revealing it to him and asking him to record the revelation. Isaiah described the act of speaking in other tongues as "stammering lips and another tongue." And described the speaking as a "rest with which You may cause the weary to rest" and a "refreshing"! God has provided a way for Spirit-filled believers to receive a rest and refreshing when communicating with Him – praying in the Spirit! Isn't that what 1 Corinthians 4:4 and Jude 20 are communicating to us? Hallelujah! Why wouldn't we want to do this often?

Praying with the Spirit

The great Apostle Paul brings out one of the tremendous benefits of praying in tongues in 1 Corinthians 14:14-15, "For if I pray in a tongue, my spirit prays, but my understanding is unfruitful. What is the conclusion then? I will pray with the spirit, and I will also pray with the understanding. I will sing with the spirit, and I will also sing with the understanding." When a born-again, Spirit-filled believer prays in an unknown tongue the utterance comes from his/her spirit. This is why the understanding is unfruitful. The utterance is not originating in our mind; it is originating in our spirit. Our born-again spirit has the mind of Christ. 1 Corinthians 2:16 tells us, "For who has known the mind of the Lord that he may instruct Him? But we have the mind of Christ." This is an awesome statement!

Our physical brain is limited and certainly does not know everything. There are many scriptures which make this point, including the very context of Paul's statement here. Yet, in our new born-again spirit, we are a completely new creature (2 Cor. 5:17). We actually have the mind of Christ. The spirit of a born-again man has been renewed in knowledge after the image of Him that created him (Col. 3:10). We have received an anointing in our spirit so that we know all things (1 John 2:20). Praise God! So, the spiritual portion of a Christian has the mind of Christ while our physical brain does not. (Wommack, "1 & 2 Corinthians" 870, footnote 6).

All other types of prayer, such as the prayer of supplication and petition, or the prayer of agreement or thanksgiving, all come from or through our mind. Praying with tongues bypasses the mind. It does not bypass the will; the will is involved in that you must be willing to cooperate with God by faith and speak forth the utterance from your spirit as it processes through your soul. Your soul is your mind, will and emotions. The will is involved but the understanding is unfruitful. Verse fifteen gives an awesome insight. Paul said, I will pray with the spirit, and I will pray with the understanding." We can shift back and forth praying with our spirit, then praying with the understanding. I would imagine that most Spirit-filled Christians have experienced this. There have been times when I wanted to pray over a situation involving a family member but did not know all the details of the situation. I can pray for a few minutes out of my own understanding and intellect based upon my knowledge but quickly exhaust my understanding of the situation. I can then shift over into the spirit and begin to pray in tongues. After a time of praying in the spirit something will come to mind. Then I shift right back into my understanding, praying in English again. In this way the Holy Spirit can work with me overcoming the limitations of my mind to help me accomplish the will of God in prayer.

It Helps Our Weakness

This is beautifully expressed in Romans 8:26-27:

Likewise, the Spirit also helps in our weaknesses. For we do not know what we should pray for as we ought, but the Spirit Himself makes intercession for us with groanings which cannot be uttered. Now He who searches the hearts knows what the mind of the Spirit is, because He makes intercession for the saints according to the will of God.

We have all experienced times when we do not know how to pray as we ought simply because we are limited by our knowledge or finite brains. This verse tells us the Spirit helps us in our weaknesses. The word "helps" comes from the Greek word *sunantilambanomai* which is defined as; "to take hold of opposite together, i.e., cooperate, help". (Strong's #4878). This communicates a powerful truth to us. When we are praying and come to the place where we no longer know what to say or to pray as we ought, the Holy Spirit will help us by making intercession for us, or with us. It says the "Spirit also helps in our weakness..." When we shift over into the spirit and begin to pray in another tongue the Spirit "takes hold of opposite together" with us; He helps us by shouldering the load with us and helps to move the mountain with us! Praise God! Verse twenty-seven tells us the Spirit makes intercession for the saints according to the will of God. When we pray in the spirit we are praying the perfect will of God. Kenneth E. Hagin shared his insight on this:

Praying in other tongues is praying in line with God's perfect will. The Holy Ghost not only knows what God's will is, but He will also never lead us away from the Word. That means as we yield to the Holy Spirit and allow Him to help us pray, He will always lead us in line with what God has said. (Tongues Beyond 173).

You may be facing a problem you feel you can't handle and don't even know how to pray. When you begin to pray in tongues, the Holy Spirit helps you and prays through you according to the will of God! When your understanding is exhausted, the Holy Spirit makes up the difference. With the Holy Spirit as your intercessor you can't lose! There are only two kinds of problems you can have: the kind where you know how to pray and the kind where you don't know how to pray. With this verse, we have them both covered! If you know how to pray, then pray with the understanding. If you don't know how to pray, pray in tongues. And know the Holy Spirit is helping you according to the perfect will of God! Amen!

A Prayer and Praise Language

The Apostle makes a reference to another important truth which occurs when the believer prays in tongues; that is, we give thanks well! Notice 1 Corinthians 14:15-17:

> What is the conclusion then? I will pray with the spirit, and I will also pray with the understanding. I will sing with the spirit, and I will also sing with the understanding. Otherwise, if you bless with the spirit, how will he who occupies the place of the uninformed say "Amen" at your giving of thanks, since he does not understand what you say? For you indeed give thanks well, but the other is not edified.

The psalmist said, "I will bless the Lord at all times; His praise shall continually be in my mouth." (Ps. 34.1). Praise, worship, and thanksgiving are things God has ordained for all day long, and at all times. Praying in tongues is one way to do that. Paul said when you speak in other tongues you "give thanks well". This is a way to give thanks to God from our spirit! What an awesome way to thank Him for our salvation, healing, or deliverance. What an awesome way to express our thanks and faith in His faithfulness to supply all our need according to His riches in glory! (Phil. 4.19). Kenneth E. Hagin commented on this:

Of course, it's still good for us to give thanks to God by praying in tongues. In fact, verse 17 says, "For thou verily givest thanks WELL." Paul is saying here that giving thanks in tongues provides the most perfect way to pray and to give thanks, especially when we are by ourselves. (Tongues Beyond 207).

The reference in verse fifteen to "praying with the spirit" and "singing with the spirit" are describing praying and singing in tongues. It is clear from the use of a lower case "s" in the word spirit, that this is a reference to our human spirit, not the Holy Spirit. Since we are singing and praying from our spirit we aren't experiencing the hindrances which we would get from our mind. We are giving perfect praise unto God without the limitations of our human language or thought!

A Relationship Function

The basic purpose of prayer in general is that it is a relationship function. Prayer should not be viewed as a religious exercise. It should be personal and intimate communication with our Father. Often when we hear people pray it is like they become a different person. They will use King James English or various tones in their voice which is not common to their everyday language. Prayer is a way of communicating and fellowshipping with our Father. It is one of the primary ways of getting to know Him personally and intimately. We develop close relationship with Him as we speak to Him and He with us. Our devotional prayer language, praying in other tongues, is part of that. The Holy Spirit is assisting us in a significant way as we spend time with our Father fellowshipping with Him in tongues.

There are two brief mentions in the Book of Acts pertaining to this. The first is found in Acts chapter two, verse eleven: "Cretans and Arabs – we hear them speaking in our own tongues the wonderful works of God." This is in reference to the crowd's response on the Day of Pentecost when the Holy Spirit was initially poured out. This international gathering of Jews heard the Galileans speaking in various languages which were understood by those hearers. We're not told everything that was being spoken, but we are told they were speaking the "wonderful works of God". This is praise to God. We worship God for who He is. He is our God, so He deserves our worship! We praise our God for what He has done. Devotional tongues are a praise to our God. We praise Him from our spirit as the Holy Spirit gives us utterance. And you don't have to be a Bible scholar to do this. The most immature Spirit-filled believer among us can do this. When we exercise this gift we extol the greatness of our God!

The second brief mention from the Book of Acts I want to point out is found in Acts chapter ten, verse forty-six, "For they heard them speak with tongues and magnify God." This took place when Cornelius' family and friends were filled with the Spirit. We're told, as they spoke in tongues they magnified God! Magnify means to make great, to enlarge or increase. When we magnify something it looks larger to us. I own a good pair of binoculars which will magnify up to thirty power. If I were to use them to look across the room over a congregation to focus in on an object on the far wall, the object is enlarged in my view. It becomes so big that it fills my view. The congregation is still seated before me, but I can't see them in the optic because it is focused on another object which is now the focus of my attention. When we pray in tongues it directs all of our focus on God and He is enlarged to us! God gets "bigger" so to speak. In actuality this doesn't increase God's size; it just causes us to bring things back into perspective. God is bigger than all our problems, bigger than all our fears, bigger than any mountain that we can or cannot see! Amen! As we pray and worship in our devotional language God is enlarged to us and our problems just pale in comparison. And our faith to overcome those problems increases exponentially. We are building ourselves up on our most holy faith (Jude 20)! Why wouldn't we want to do this often? Amen.

6 OUR VICTORIOUS POSITION IN CHRIST

There is a definite reason our God has chosen to provide an empowerment for His people. It is so we may be effective representatives for Him. One reason many people live below their rights and privileges in Christ is because they fail to understand what has been provided for them in their relationship with God. The Kingdom of God is unlike any earthly kingdom in that the most outstanding element distinguishing the Kingdom of God from every other kingdom is the concept that every citizen of heaven is personally related to the King! Which means, every person in the kingdom is of the royal lineage! Let's notice how the great Apostle Peter stated it in his writings in 1 Peter 2:4-10:

> Coming to Him as to a living stone, rejected indeed by men, but chosen by God and precious, you also, as living stones, are being built up a spiritual house, a holy priesthood, to offer up spiritual sacrifices acceptable to God through Jesus Christ. Therefore, it is also contained in the Scripture, "Behold, I lay in Zion a chief cornerstone, elect, precious, and he who believes on Him will by no means be put to shame." Therefore, to you who believe, He is precious; but to those who are disobedient, "The stone which the builders rejected has

become the chief cornerstone," and "A stone of stumbling and a rock of offense." They stumble, being disobedient to the word, to which they also were appointed. But you are a chosen generation, a royal priesthood, a holy nation, His own special people, that you may proclaim the praises of Him who called you out of darkness into His marvelous light; who once were not a people but are now the people of God, who had not obtained mercy but now have obtained mercy.

These verses tell us Jesus was the stone which the builders rejected. He came to His own, but His own didn't receive Him. Religion put Him on the cross! But God had plans for the "stone that was rejected." God raised Him up and made Him the "chief cornerstone", and now every believer who comes to Christ becomes a "living stone" added to the kingdom! Verse nine describes our heritage as believers. We have become a chosen generation, a royal priesthood, a holy nation, God's own special people! Our Father had a long-held desire for His own special people and through Jesus He fulfilled His desire! Described beautifully in verse ten, "who once were not a people but are now the people of God, who had not obtained mercy but now have obtained mercy." Praise God, what a wonderful truth! As God's own special people we have been given a specific function of representing God's nature and character before the world. Let's notice specifically we are the "people of God", not a nation of subjects, but rather, sons! We are people of royal lineage tasked with the responsibility of representing Him and His government on the earth. It is important to understand God's purpose in this. God is not interested in having subjects in His kingdom; He wants only children, royal heirs to His domain. As is brought out in Romans 8:16-17, "The Spirit Himself bears witness with our spirit that we are children of God, and if children, then heirs—heirs of God and joint heirs with Christ, if indeed we suffer with *Him*, that we may also be glorified together."

God's purpose in sending Jesus was not to establish religion. Organized religion was a problem. He wanted relationship with man by establishing a family of spiritual sons through which He would accomplish His purpose in the earth. Which brings us to our role in the Kingdom of God. God desires to influence the earth from heaven through mankind. He has chosen to work through mankind to minister His love and goodness to the world.

Ambassadors for Christ

"Ambassador" is the term chosen by the Apostle Paul in 2 Corinthians 5:20 to designate those chosen by God to represent Him: "Now then, we are ambassadors for Christ, as though God were pleading through us: we implore *you* on Christ's behalf, be reconciled to God." As believers in Christ we are ambassadors for Him! We don't have to ask for it or obtain it some other way, it is bestowed upon us. Therefore, we must understand what it means to be Christ's ambassadors. Both for the purpose of representing Him well and so we can operate in the privileges associated with being His representatives! First let's understand, there is no such thing as some Christians being called as ambassadors and not others. If you are a Christian, you are an ambassador for Christ! Next, there is no such thing as a part-time ambassador. We are ambassadors at work, we are ambassadors at home. We are ambassadors at church and during recreation times. In order to be effective at this, it is important to understand what this entails. Dr. Myles Munroe shared this insight:

An ambassador is a unique political creature in all kingdoms and his disposition must be understood fully, in order to appreciate the power and distinction of this revered position. Here are some very paramount qualities of an ambassador:

- Appointed by the king, not voted into position
- Appointed to represent the state or kingdom
- Committed only to the state's interests
- Embodies the nation-state or kingdom
- Totally covered by the state
- Is the responsibility of the state
- Never becomes a citizen of the state or kingdom to which he is assigned
- Can only be recalled by the king or president
- Has access to all his nation's wealth for assignment
- Never speaks his personal position on any issue, only his nation's official position
- His goal is to influence the territory for his kingdom government. (Rediscovering the Kingdom 110-111).

Every nation appoints ambassadors to represent its interests to other nations; the Kingdom of God is no different. God chose to communicate His will throughout the earth through personal representatives which He calls ambassadors, not through religion. By definition, an ambassador is a representative of a ruling authority. He is a high-ranking minister of state sent forth to represent his own country. An ambassador is not sent forth to speak their own personal opinions, but only the official policies of the government which appointed them.

I know of a preacher who went on a mission trip to preach in Russia. He is a very joyful, excited, over-the-top personality who is very expressive in his preaching. He was invited to speak at a particular meeting. When he arrived, an interpreter was provided for him. When he took the platform, he began by excitedly saying, "Praise the Lord!" The interpreter repeated the phrase in the Russian language, but in a slow, monotone voice. The preacher looked at him and repeated,

"Praise the Lord!" Again, the interpreter responded with little expression. The preacher then spoke directly to the interpreter and said, "Listen. You're here to interpret for me, you represent me. You're supposed to say what I say and act how I act!" When he said that, the Spirit of God spoke to him from within, "That's exactly what I want from My people!" That's what an ambassador does; he represents, he speaks for another. As we are about our Father's business there are some Biblical truths which apply to us as Christ's ambassadors.

Citizens of Their Home Country

The first distinction I want to discuss is ambassadors are citizens of their home country. An ambassador is not a citizen of the country he is sent to. He is a citizen of the country he is from. The Apostle Paul said, "For our citizenship is in heaven, from which we also eagerly wait for the Savior, the Lord Jesus Christ." (Phil. 3.20). Jesus taught the same principle in John 15:19, "If you were of the world, the world would love its own. Yet because you are not of the world, but I chose you out of the world, therefore the world hates you." Although we are in the world, we are not supposed to be of this world. As I have said many times, there should be something different about us. Unfortunately, sad to say, many times there is little difference between the believer and the unbeliever who lives next door. There should be more victory in our lives, more peace, more health, more energy, etc.

I have served as a prison Chaplain in Texas for sixteen years. The part of this ministry I love is I that have the privilege of preaching the Good News. Unfortunately, the part I don't love is, I am often responsible for giving the men bad news from home. If there has been a critical illness or a death in the family, those messages come to me to deliver. I've observed how different men handle it. Some break down. Sometimes it is a man who attends my services where I faithfully preach these truths of victorious Christian living. Too often I see those men fall apart like they have never heard the Word of faith. It takes all of about two seconds to see who is applying their faith and who is not. I always try to communicate that the first report is not the last report! I like to share Isaiah 53:1, "Who has believed our report? And to whom has the arm of the Lord been revealed?" The phrase, "arm of the Lord" is a reference to God's redemptive power. I like to turn this verse around to think of it like this: The arm of the Lord is revealed to those who believe the report of the Lord. We often are too quick to believe the negative report. In a time of crisis, I like to tell people, "It matters what you believe right now. Believe the report of the Lord. Don't act like it's not true, act like it is true!" That's what kingdom citizens do.

This idea that we are in the world but not of the world was a philosophy held by people of God from the past. An example of it is found in Hebrews 11:13-16:

> These all died in faith, not having received the promises, but having seen them afar off were assured of them, embraced them and confessed that they were strangers and pilgrims on the earth. For those who say such things declare plainly that they seek a homeland. And truly if they had called to mind that country from which they had come out, they would have had opportunity to return. But now they desire a better, that is, a heavenly country. Therefore, God is not ashamed to be called their God, for He has prepared a city for them.

Our love for our King and His kingdom should be the dominant pursuit of our lives with the understanding, our true homeland is a heavenly country. Paul was addressing the elders from Ephesus when he said:

But none of these things move me; nor do I count my life dear to myself, so that I may finish my race with joy, and the ministry which I received from the Lord Jesus, to testify to the gospel of the grace of God. (Acts 20.24)

The key to finishing our race with joy in this life is not counting our lives dear to ourselves. To be honest, I love my life and I believe God wants us to have lives we love and find fulfilling. We should never forget that true joy is found in our relationship with Jesus! Matthew 16:24-25 tells us: "Then Jesus said to His disciples, 'If anyone desires to come after Me, let him deny himself, and take up his cross, and follow Me. For whoever desires to save his life will lose it, but whoever loses his life for My sake will find it.'" It's in losing our lives in Jesus that we really find the joy of what God intended life to be. It is certainly acceptable to love our lives, but we should not hold our lives more dearly than our love for Jesus or the desire to finish our race and the assignment we have received from Him.

Authorized by Their Home Country

Ambassadors don't stand in their own name; they stand in the name of the one they represent! This is a tremendously important point to understand if we want to operate in victory and flow in the power of God. When an ambassador brings a message into a nation from the homeland they have all of the power and authority of the homeland behind them! I have made a few brief references to this prior to this chapter, but a bit more explanation will be helpful. I will begin with Matthew's account of the Great Commission:

And Jesus came and spoke to them, saying, 'All authority has been given to Me in heaven and on earth. Go therefore and make disciples of all the nations, baptizing them in the name of the Father and of the Son and of the Holy Spirit, teaching them to observe all things that I have commanded you; and lo, I am with you always, even to the end of the age.' Amen. (Matt. 28.18-20).

In this account, Jesus began by saying, "All authority has been given to Me…" Most people can understand this; even worldly people acknowledge that Jesus was operating in power and authority as He healed the sick, cast out devils, and raised the dead. A brief summary of events is given by Andrew Wommack:

> God had delegated the power over the earth to mankind from the beginning (Gen 1:26-28; Ps. 8:4-8; 115:16). When man disobeyed God (Gen 3:1-6), that power was delivered to Satan (Lk. 4:6). Therefore, the Lord did not have absolute control over the earth and its affairs. When Jesus died, He descended into hell (Ps. 16:10 with Acts 2:31; Eph. 4:8-10) and stripped Satan of all his power (Rev. 1:18). Now God once again has all power in heaven and earth. The reason we can go into all the world and share the gospel is because Jesus now has all power in heaven and earth, and as His ambassadors (2 Cor. 5:20), we have that power too. (Gospels Edition 504, footnotes 3 and 4).

In these verses in Matthew twenty-eight, Jesus delegated His authority to the Church. Authority can be defined as the "right to act". Authority, that is, the right to act has been given by God to man. In the New Testament there are several Greek words used for power; I want to discuss two of them. The first one, important for us to be familiar with is the Greek word *dunamis*. Strong's Exhaustive Concordance defines it as: "miraculous power, ability, abundance, might, power, strength." (Strong's #1411). It is the root word from which we derive our English words "dynamic", "dynamite" and "dynamo". Acts 1:8 is an example of its usage, "But you shall receive power (dunamis) when the Holy Spirit is come upon you…" This clearly speaks of the presence and anointing of the Holy Spirit as being the power source in a believer's life. Another good example is found in Acts 10:38, "How God anointed Jesus of Nazareth with the Holy Spirit and with power, who went about doing good and healing all who were oppressed by the devil, for God was with Him." It was the anointing power of the Holy Spirit that worked miracles in the life of Jesus. According to Jesus' words, we can expect to accomplish the same miraculous works if we believe, "Most assuredly, I say to you, he who believes in Me, the works that I do he will do also; and greater works than these he will do, because I go to my Father." (Jn. 14.12).

The next Greek word I will discuss is the word *exousia*. Strong's Exhaustive Concordance defines it as "privilege, freedom, delegated influence, authority." (Strong's #1849). So we understand that exousia is delegated authority and liberty to exercise the full power of attorney in God's interests. Matthew 28:18 is an example of its usage. From the King James Version, it reads, "And Jesus came and spoke to them, saying, 'All power (exousia) is given unto Me in heaven and in earth." The New King James Version actually renders this, "All authority has been given to Me..." Luke 10:19 is a verse which actually employs both words, "Behold, I give you the authority (exousia) to trample on all the power (dunamis) of the enemy, and nothing shall by any means hurt you." This verse makes it clear from Jesus' words that we have been given authority over all the power of the enemy! And now it is incumbent upon us to be willing to use this authority to enforce the victory that has been provided for us! Man was born, and now born again, to win under God and over the devil and his works. Laying hands on the sick, casting out devils, and speaking with tongues are examples of Kingdom ministry every ambassador is authorized to perform. You can have confidence to know you stand in His name as His representative to minister with power!

Signs and Wonders Necessary

I want to emphasize the importance of ambassadors for Christ operating in power. Hebrews 2:1-4 shows us this:

> Therefore we must give the more earnest heed to the things we have heard, lest we drift away. For if the word spoken through angels proved steadfast, and every transgression and disobedience received a just reward, how shall we escape if we neglect so great a salvation, which at the first began to be spoken by the Lord, and was confirmed to us by those who heard Him, God also bearing witness both with signs and wonders, with various miracles, and gifts of the Holy Spirit, according to His own will?

Notice this says the message the Lord spoke was confirmed to us. Verse four tells us God bore witness to Jesus' ministry with signs, wonders, miracles and gifts of the Holy Spirit. Even Jesus had to have this message confirmed in order to validate His ministry. It's a mistake to think miracles aren't necessary for us today. Another reference is found in John 5:36 where Jesus said, "But, I have a greater witness than John's; for the works which the Father has given Me to finish – the very works that I do bear witness of Me, that the Father has sent Me." In this chapter the Jews persecuted Jesus and sought to kill Him because He healed the man of his illness at the pool of Bethesda on the Sabbath day. Basically they were saying to Him, "Who are You and what makes You someone we should listen to? Why should we believe You?" Jesus' answer is in verse thirty-six. He said the works He did, the miracles, wonders and signs; the blind eyes opened, deaf ears unstopped, the lame being healed all served as a witness to Him and were a reason to believe Him! His ministry was validated by God's power operating through Him! Jesus said this very thing another time which is recorded in John 10:37-38: "If I do not do the works of My

Father, do not believe Me; but if I do, though you do not believe Me, believe the works, that you may know and believe that the Father *is* in Me, and I in Him."

Essentially Jesus was saying, "If I don't have the actions to back up what I'm saying, then don't believe Me! But if I do, then believe!" The power operating in Jesus' ministry was a confirmation that His message was from God! If Jesus and the early Church had to have their message confirmed by the power of the Holy Spirit, how much more do we need the same confirmation? It is arrogant and inaccurate to assume we are greater than Jesus or the Apostles and don't need the power of the Holy Spirit to confirm our message. The true preaching of God's Word should be confirmed with signs, wonders, and miracles!

Ambassadors are authorized by the one they represent. This is why we have been given the right to use the name of Jesus! Many people in the Church desire miracles, or even desperately need a miracle, but they approach it wrong. Rather than acknowledging and recognizing that God has empowered us and given us the legal right to use His name and His Word to enforce the victory which has already been won, they beg God to do what He's authorized us to do. Often people will pray, cry out, and beg God to heal or pour out His Spirit, but they are failing to realize God has done these things for us through Jesus. It's not His turn to move; it's our turn to believe and act on His Word! The average Christian believes God can do anything. But the average Christian also fails to acknowledge what God has already done and that He has empowered us to accomplish His will by faith.

The great mistake of the Church today is she has tried to advance the Kingdom in word only. The mark of a true Christian should not be just what we say; it should also be demonstrated by the power of the Holy Spirit. I know this is different than what many people have heard and believe. Many would consider this radical, odd, or an unusual view of Christianity. But when we study the Book of Acts this is what we see in the early Church. The Book of Acts Christianity shouldn't be odd or unusual; it should be normal Christianity. Not just for the Pentecostal or Charismatic Christians, but for everyone. Unfortunately, it is odd or unusual to many, but it shouldn't be.

I don't want anyone who reads this to feel condemned by my words. Someone might ask, "Do you mean I have to make this happen in my own strength?" No, not in our own ability or human strength. Understand it is out of the power that resides on the inside of your born-again spirit, God's power inside of you! Ephesians 3:20, "Now to Him who is able to do exceedingly, abundantly above all that we ask or think, according to the power that works in us..." The average Christian thinks God's power is in heaven, but this verse tells us His power works in us! We have access to His power through His name. We pray to the Father in the name of Jesus. We use the name of Jesus to cast out demons or heal the sick. It's God's power available to us in Jesus' name!

The Word of God has power and authority! Hebrews 4:12 says:

> For the Word of God is living and powerful, and sharper than any two-edged sword, piercing even to the division of soul and spirit, and of joints and marrow, and is a discerner of the thoughts and intents of the heart.

The Word by the Spirit can do all the person of Jesus can do! Someone might say, "Oh brother, the Word has to be quickened to you before you can act on it." I say, the Word is already quickened. It's alive and powerful. It's just waiting to be believed! That's why God gave it to us, so we can act on it! Romans 10:30 says, "For whoever calls on the name of the Lord shall be saved." Can we act on that scripture? Of course we can! 1 John 1:9 tells us, "If we confess our sins, He is faithful and just to forgive us our sins and to cleanse us from all unrighteousness." Can we act on that scripture? Of course we can! Philippians 4:13, "I can do all things through Christ who strengthens me" is just waiting to be believed and acted upon. Never forget that your attitude toward the Word is your attitude toward Jesus. Because Jesus is the living Word according to John 1:1, "In the beginning was the Word, and the Word was with God, and the Word was God." And verse fourteen, "And the Word became flesh and dwelt among us..." We have been authorized as ambassadors by His Spirit and by His Word! Amen!

Supported by Their Home Country

An ambassador doesn't live off of the economy of the country he is in; he lives off the economy of the country he is from. The government of the home country is responsible for the support of their ambassador as he serves in that capacity. As an ambassador for Christ we live on God's economy! It doesn't matter if this world's economy is up or down; this world's system is not our source – God is our source. He is our provider. Often I tell people God could have set this up another way. He could have arranged it so every time a person confesses Jesus as Lord and becomes born again, instantly millions of dollars suddenly appears in their bank account and they are set financially for the rest of their lives! My flesh really likes the sound of that! The reason God didn't set it up to happen this way is because He wants us to trust Him and be dependent upon Him as our source and not our bank account. Don't misunderstand my comment. I believe God wants us to prosper. 3 John 2 tells us, "Beloved, I pray that you may prosper in all things and be in health, just as your soul prospers." God's will for us is to prosper and live in health, and we will to the degree we prosper our souls. Amen! It's important to rightly divide the word of truth (2 Tim. 2.15) in order to understand God's will for our lives in this area. As our souls prosper in the areas of health and prosperity, faith rises in us to receive it because faith comes by hearing, and hearing by the Word of God (Rom. 10.17). Dr. Myles Munroe articulated this well:

> We should not focus on other things even in our prayers, but our concentration should be on the will of God and the coming of His kingdom. An ambassador's home government provides him with everything he needs to live and perform his official function: office, home, car, staff, funding, etc. In the same way, as we seek God's kingdom and His righteousness as our first priority, He will supply everything we need for daily living and accomplishing His will. If we set ourselves to handling our King's business, He will handle ours. It is a relationship of faith, trust, and obedience, enabling us to exercise power and authority in His name. Such faith grows from an increasing understanding of our position as ambassadors of Christ. (Rediscovering the Kingdom 148-149).

We must learn to trust God completely as our source. This means, our job isn't our source, our bank account isn't our source, government programs aren't our source or, God forbid, our credit card isn't our source! Jobs may change, bank accounts may fail, government systems may come and go but God will never fail us! God's economy is always constant; it's never up and down. This is one reason we give offerings and tithes. By tithing the first fruits of our income we are saying things to God. We say thank you to Him by giving to Him, we worship Him with our gifts, and we say we are trusting Him each time we give the tithe of our income. Don't give the leftovers but put Him first in your financial life. Matthew 6:33 tells us, "But seek first the kingdom of God and His righteousness, and all these things shall be added to you." God has made the way for all of our needs to be met by seeking Him first. We are to seek His kingdom first, not things. God has made it so that when we seek Him first, things we need come to us as a by-product of putting the Kingdom and His righteousness as the priority in our lives!

A really good scriptural example of this is found in the Old Testament story of the children of Israel leaving Egypt. They had to stop trusting in the ways of Egypt, and start trusting in the ways of God. And so do we! Egypt is a type of the world's system. We are in the world, but we are not of the world. We must resist the temptation to become too comfortable simply trusting in this world's system of natural supply. After four hundred-thirty years of Egyptian bondage, God sent Moses and Aaron to the Pharaoh to accomplish the Jews' deliverance. Pharaoh urged Israel to leave Egypt after the death of his firstborn resulting from the tenth plague. Exodus 12:31 says, "Then he called for Moses and Aaron by night and said, 'Rise, go out from among my people, both you and the children of Israel. And go serve the Lord as you have said.'" After four hundred-thirty years of captivity the Israelites made their way out of Egypt toward the land promised them. "So God led the people around by the way of the wilderness of the Red Sea. And the children of Israel went up in orderly ranks out of the land of Egypt." (Ex. 13.18). For forty years Israel would be completely dependent upon God to provide their food, water, and protection. Whenever I read this account I'm always struck by the fact that although God worked powerfully to deliver, sustain and protect them from new enemies, Israel reacted with fear, disbelief, and murmuring.

> And they journeyed from Elim, and all the congregation of the children of Israel came to the Wilderness of Sin, which is between Elim and Sinai, on the fifteenth day of the second month after they departed from the land of Egypt. Then the whole congregation of the children of

Israel complained against Moses and Aaron in the wilderness. And the children of Israel said to them, "Oh, that we had died by the hand of the Lord in the land of Egypt, when we sat by the pots of meat and when we ate bread to the full! For You have brought us out into this wilderness to kill this whole assembly with hunger. (Ex. 16.1-3).

Although God had brought them out of Egypt, Egypt was still in them! How quickly they had forgotten the years of bondage but remembered the *supposed* security! The children of Israel had to learn to stop trusting in Egypt for their provision and begin to trust God for their provision. In spite of their grumbling, God made the bitter water sweet (Ex. 15.22-26); He miraculously provided food (Ex. 16.1-36) and water (Ex. 17.3-7). We can learn, and begin to trust Him completely to provide and protect us as well. This is clearly communicated to us from the New Testament.

My God Shall Supply

Let's look at a tremendous promise from Philippians 4:19, "And my God shall supply all your need according to His riches in glory by Christ Jesus." Remember, as citizens of heaven we live off of God's economy. Some basic, but most important truths are being emphasized in this short but relevant scripture. First, God is our provider! We work at our jobs or vocations to earn a paycheck but, let's never forget neither this world's economy, our jobs, nor bank accounts are our source. Although we are investing our time, skills, and abilities to earn our pay, ultimately we know God has given us the ability, intelligence, and health to be productive and earn our salaries. As citizens of the Kingdom, the King is personally responsible for our provision and well-being! What comfort, confidence and assurance this gives to know we have God's unfailing Word promising to care for us in this way!

He Provides All Our Need

Another basic, but most important truth emphasized here is our God supplies all our need! Not some, not most, but all of our need. Another New Testament passage which supports this is found in Matthew 6:25-34:

> Therefore I say to you, do not worry about your life, what you will eat or what you will drink; nor about your body, what you will put on. Is not life more than food and the body more than clothing? Look at the birds of the air, for they neither sow nor reap nor gather into barns; yet your heavenly Father feeds them. Are you not of more value than they? Which of you by worrying can add one cubit to his stature?

> So why do you worry about clothing? Consider the lilies of the field, how they grow: they neither toil nor spin; and yet I say to you that even Solomon in all his glory was not arrayed like one of these. Now if God so clothes the grass of the field, which today is, and tomorrow is thrown into the oven, will He not much more clothe you, O you of little faith?

> Therefore do not worry, saying, 'What shall we eat?' or 'What shall we drink?' or 'What shall we wear?' For after all these things the Gentiles seek. For your heavenly Father knows that you need all these things. But seek first the kingdom of God and His righteousness, and all these things shall be added to you. Therefore, do not worry about tomorrow, for tomorrow will worry about its own things. Sufficient for the day is its own trouble.

In this passage Jesus is dealing with single-hearted devotion to God, as is stated in verse twenty-four, "No one can serve two masters; for either he will hate the one and love the other, or else he will be loyal to the one and despise the other.

You cannot serve God and Mammon." He uses the birds of the air and lilies of the field as illustrations to show God's faithfulness to care for His creation. How much more will He provide for us? I particularly like the way verse thirty-one reads in the King James Version, "Therefore take no thought, saying, 'What shall we eat?' or 'What shall we drink?' or 'Wherewithal shall we be clothed?'" Andrew Wommack shares this insight:

> The way we take or receive an anxious thought is by speaking it. Doubtful thoughts will come, but it is not sin until we entertain them. According to this verse, speaking forth these thoughts is one way of entertaining them; therefore, don't speak forth these negative thoughts. (Gospels Edition 83, footnote 44).

Jesus is emphasizing that anxiety and worry about provision is unnecessary and unfruitful for any Christian because we have an unfailing Covenant promise from our heavenly Father to provide our every need. Verse thirty-two is interesting; Jesus makes the comment, "For after all these things the Gentiles seek." The reference to "Gentiles" refers to the Jewish understanding that they were heathen or non-covenant people. This is described in Ephesians 2:11-12:

> Therefore remember that you, once Gentiles in the flesh—who are called Uncircumcision by what is called the Circumcision made in the flesh by hands— that at that time you were without Christ, being aliens from the commonwealth of Israel and strangers from the covenants of promise, having no hope and without God in the world.

These verses graphically describe the complete hopelessness of all Gentiles before Jesus opened the door of salvation to them. The word "uncircumcision" is a reference to these people who were without covenant with God, "having no hope and without God in the world." Verse thirteen describes the total transformation which took place, "But now in Christ Jesus you who once were far off have been brought near by the blood of Christ."

So Jesus' comment in Matthew 6:32, "For after all these things the Gentiles seek" shows us the priorities of the non-covenant people. People who are not in covenant with God seek after things, what to eat, what to wear, where to live. As covenant people, citizens of heaven, we are not to seek after things. We are to seek God first. As we do, the things we need, food, clothing, and shelter are added to us as a by-product of putting God first! He's El Shaddai, the God who is more than enough! He not only can provide for us; He *will* provide for us. And He'll do better than you can do for yourself! Amen!

His Riches in Glory

Another basic, but important truth brought out in Philippians 4:19 is He provides according to His riches in glory. He doesn't meet our need according to the riches on earth, it's not according to this world's economy, or even our employer. Our provision is according to His riches in glory. It will help to put this in perspective. Revelation chapter twenty-one gives a description of the New Jerusalem. Verses eighteen and nineteen say, "The construction of its wall was of jasper: and the city was pure gold, like clear glass. The foundations of the wall of the city were adorned with all kinds of precious stones…" Verse twenty-one continues, "The twelve gates were twelve pearls: each individual gate was of one pearl. And the street of the city was pure gold, like transparent glass". This is a picture of super abundance! Gold is so precious to us that we take small portions of it and fashion it into fine jewelry. But in heaven the streets are paved with it!

My father died and went to heaven in 2012 after spending most of his life running heavy equipment in road construction. He enjoyed his work. I don't know if there is a need for road maintenance in the New Jerusalem, but if there is I can just imagine my dad being involved overseeing the work. If there is a pothole in the street I can imagine dad backing an asphalt truck in to make the repair, when God's audible voice gently speaks, "Charlie, what are you doing?" Dad replies, "I'm repairing this street!" "We don't use asphalt on our streets here," replies God. Dad: "Oh, that's right, let's bring in the concrete." "No, concrete won't do either" says the Lord. Of course, I'm just playing by imagining like this. The point is, there is so much abundance in God's economy that meeting our miniscule need is no problem for our generous God! An ambassador for Christ should not have a poverty mentality! God can, and will take good care of us.

Protected by the Home Country

Although an Ambassador is assigned to a certain country, he is protected by the laws governing the country he is from. To attack an ambassador or an embassy is a direct attack against the home country. An ambassador can expect to be protected by the home government. There are many stories in the Bible of God protecting and delivering His people. One could spend a long time discussing and studying various examples, but let it suffice for me to mention just a few; Daniel in the lion's den, Shadrack, Meshack, and Abednego in the fiery furnace. But, even more significant for us to consider is the provision made by Jesus on Calvary's cross. All that has been purchased for us through redemption is now made available by grace. What God offers us by grace must be received by faith. We access God's divine protection by faith, that is, by believing and speaking the promises. As has been mentioned previously, there should be more victory in believers' lives. 1 John 4:4 tells us, "You are of God little children, and have overcome them: because greater is He that is in you, than he that is in the world." It should be common practice for us as believers, when we experience challenges, trials, or even crisis situations to confess these truths: "I am a victor; I'm more than a conqueror. The Greater One lives in me and makes me a success. I can do all things through Christ!" Too often, even Christians have the attitude "There's nothing I can do.", or "I'm just a man." And just accept defeat as though there is no recourse. No, our God is our help; He is our strength! Psalm 27:1, "The Lord is my light and my salvation; who shall I fear? The Lord is the strength of my life; of whom shall I be afraid?"

Sent with a Message

Ambassadors are sent with a message from the home country. The message we are to take to the world is communicated to us in 2 Corinthians 5:18-21:

> Now all things are of God, who has reconciled us to Himself through Jesus Christ, and has given us the ministry of reconciliation, that is, that God was in Christ reconciling the world to Himself, not imputing their trespasses to them, and has committed to us the word of reconciliation. Now then, we are ambassadors for Christ, as though God were pleading through us: we implore you on Christ's behalf, be reconciled to God. For He made Him who knew no sin to be sin for us, that we might become the righteousness of God in Him.

The message of Christ's ambassador is to preach the gospel of reconciliation. We have been sent to tell the world God isn't angry with them, nor is He holding their sin against them. This is the good news the world doesn't know. Sinners think God is angry. They perceive Him as just waiting to punish them for their sin. It's our responsibility to tell them Jesus didn't die for the sins of the Church, He died for the sins of the world. Romans 5:6 tells us, "For when we were still without strength, in due time Christ died for the ungodly."

Unfortunately, today there are people who believe God will not fellowship with sinners or that He will not hear them when they pray. But this is inconsistent with Jesus' ministry. Matthew 9:10 records, "Now it happened as Jesus sat at the table in the house, that behold, many tax collectors and sinners came and sat down with Him and His disciples." We know Jesus didn't reject sinners. Of course the religious people didn't like it, "And when the Pharisees saw it, they said to His disciples, 'Why does your Teacher eat with tax collectors and sinners?'" (Matt. 9.11). I can hear the self-righteous, pious tone in their voices. Jesus' words in Luke 7:34 reveal the attitude of the Pharisees and lawyers rejecting the will of God, "The Son of Man has come eating and drinking, and you say, 'Look, a glutton and a winebibber, a friend of tax collectors and sinners!'" It's very interesting to me that Jesus had the reputation of being a "friend of sinners." As His ambassadors it's most important that we represent Him well to the world and communicate this message of reconciliation! As I have pointed out, 2 Corinthians 5:19 tells us Jesus came to reconcile the world to God.

Paul expounds upon this thought in Romans 5:7-8, "For scarcely for a righteous man will one die; yet perhaps for a good man someone would even dare to die. But God demonstrates His own love toward us, in that while we were still sinners, Christ died for us." We can sort of understand how a person would risk their life, or give their life for a loved one or family member. We hear stories of a mother who dives into a raging river to save her child, or a father who goes into a burning house to save his family. We can understand that. I'd take a bullet for my wife. But what I will never get over is, Jesus came to die for sinners. He gave His life for people who did not love Him, and maybe never would. What manner of Man is this? What love was demonstrated by Him! A hint of this type of love for friends is found in a story of two soldiers who fought in World War I.

World War I had settled into trench warfare when one day a young Lieutenant ordered his troops to leave the trench and attack the enemy. They cautiously climbed out of the safety of the trench and began to low-crawl across the battlefield toward the enemy when suddenly gunfire rang out. Bullets flew in almost every direction. The frightened men scurried back to the trenches and hunkered down. The battlefield fell eerily quiet, except for the moans and groans of one wounded soldier left behind on the battlefield. He was crying out for his friend, George, to come help him. George pled with the young Lieutenant to allow him to go help his friend. The Lieutenant said, "No". George didn't give up. He continued to plead for permission. The Lieutenant said, "No. I've already lost one man. I cannot afford to lose another in a foolish rescue attempt!" George wouldn't give up. He continued to beg the Lieutenant for permission. Finally, exasperated by George's requests he said, "Fine! I'm tired of listening to you. If you want to get yourself killed, go ahead!" George quickly crawled out of the trench and made his way toward his friend. He grabbed hold of him and made his way back to the trench. George rolled him over the side of the trench then fell in on top of him. But it was too late. He was already dead. The young Lieutenant screamed at George, "I told you there was no point to your bravery! You were a fool! Why did you risk your life?!" George looked up at him and replied, "I was no fool. He was alive when I got to him and the last words he spoke were, "George, I knew you would come."

That's what friends do. That's what Jesus has done for us. He hasn't left us hopeless. He didn't leave us helpless. He left the safety of heaven and came to us. Now any sinner who will put their faith in Him, will not receive judgment, wrath, or rejection. No, He came into the world to save sinners! Instead, they receive His unconditional love, grace, mercy and goodness! This is the message Christ's ambassadors have been commissioned to bring to the world. Amen!

Ambassadors Only Recalled by the Home Country

An ambassador is a political appointee assigned the responsibility of representing his or her home government. Just as an ambassador in the natural realm can only be recalled by the king or president of the home government, ambassadors for Christ will one day be recalled by our King! As Christ's ambassadors we play a key role in fulfilling what God wants accomplished in the church age, or what is also known as the Dispensation of Grace. Pastor Bob Yandian shares his insight:

> On the Day of Pentecost when the Holy Spirit was sent to dwell in man, a new administration began. The way God approaches man in our dispensation is strictly by grace. God has approached man by law. He has approached man through human government, but today God approaches man by grace. This does not mean that God was not a God of grace in the Old Testament and it does not mean that God does not have laws today. But the main way He is dealing with us is by grace. This also does not mean that God does not deal through governments today, however, again, the primary way He is dealing with the earth today is through the church and through the dispensation of grace. (Understanding the End Times 14-15).

The time will arrive when this dispensation will end. There are actually two comings of the Lord yet unfulfilled; the second coming, which is the time when Jesus returns to the earth to establish His physical kingdom and the millennial reign, and the rapture of the Church. Although the word "rapture" is not used in the Bible, we have to understand that the word is used to refer to the "catching away" of the Church which is clearly documented in the New Testament. 1 Thessalonians 4:13-18 describes this event:

> But I do not want you to be ignorant, brethren, concerning those who have fallen asleep, lest you sorrow as others who have no hope. For if we believe that Jesus died and rose again, even so God will bring with Him those who sleep in Jesus. For this we say to you by the word of the Lord, that we who are alive and remain until the coming of the Lord will by no means precede those who are asleep. For the Lord Himself will descend from heaven with a shout, with the voice of an archangel, and with the trumpet of God. And the dead in Christ will rise first. Then we who are alive and remain shall be caught up together with them in the clouds to meet the Lord in the air. And thus we shall always be with the Lord. Therefore, comfort one another with these words.

The early Church lived in the midst of the expectation that the Lord would return. It would seem Paul the Apostle looked for it to occur in his lifetime as indicated by his comment in 1 Thessalonians 4:17, "Then we who are alive and remain shall be caught up together with them in the clouds to meet the Lord in the air. And thus we shall always be with the Lord." Again, the word "rapture" is not used, but the idea of the saints being caught up, and gathered together is.

There is much talk in our modern culture about the end times, so much of which is totally unscriptural. It is not my intent to discuss the subject at length here, but some clear and proper understanding of what the Bible says concerning the end times and apocalyptic themes is necessary. Jesus made a couple of references to this subject that have been most helpful to me. Notice Matthew 24:37-42:

> But as the days of Noah were, so also will the coming of the Son of Man be. For as in the days before the flood, they were eating and drinking, marrying and giving in marriage, until the day that Noah entered the ark, and did not know until the flood came and took them all away, so also will the coming of the Son of Man be. Then two men will be in the field: one will be taken and the other left. Two women will be grinding at the mill: one will be taken and the other left. Watch therefore, for you do not know what hour your Lord is coming.

Jesus' teaching in this chapter was sparked by the disciples' question posed to Him in verse three, "Now as He sat on the Mount of Olives, the disciples came to Him privately, saying, "Tell us, when will these things be? And what will be the sign of Your coming, and of the end of the age?" Matthew recorded Jesus' response to the question through chapters twenty-four and twenty-five. Jesus prophesied that in the last days it would be as the days of Noah. People would be eating and drinking, marrying and giving in marriage, etc. In other words, it would be business as usual! So much of what we hear today paints a really scary picture. Many tend to fear the last days, but when it's viewed in light of what Jesus taught, it takes the fear out of it. I always encourage people to be careful that Hollywood is not influencing their doctrine and theology! The Bible does warn us, "in the last days perilous times will come." (2 Tim. 3.1). People will have to deal with harsh, difficult, or even dangerous times as the coming of the Lord draws near at the end of the age. But for Christ's ambassadors these are not days to be feared, they are days to be busy and fulfilling the will of God in this dispensation. We should believe for protection and provision from our Father as we walk it out by faith! Another truth Jesus spoke along these lines is found in Mark 13:32-37:

But of that day and hour no one knows, not even the angels in heaven, nor the Son, but only the Father. Take heed, watch and pray; for you do not know when the time is. It is like a man going to a far country, who left his house and gave authority to his servants, and to each his work, and commanded the doorkeeper to watch. Watch therefore, for you do not know when the master of the house is coming—in the evening, at midnight, at the crowing of the rooster, or in the morning— lest, coming suddenly, he find you sleeping. And what I say to you, I say to all: Watch!

Concerning the Lord's return Jesus taught we should be watching, we should be ready for that day, but He clearly said no one would know the day or the hour. It is pointless to speculate when He will return. I believe verse thirty-four gives us the attitude of His ambassadors; "It is like a man going to a far country, who left his house and gave authority to his servants, and to each his work, and commanded the doorkeeper to watch." Jesus likened His absence to a man going into a far country, giving authority to His servants. Although we do not know the day or hour, we are authorized and expected to be about our Father's business until He returns!

We need to be cautious and discerning when it comes to understanding the end times. There are legitimate prophecy teachers who study to show themselves approved and genuinely attempt to represent God and the Scriptures well. But there are others who only know enough about the Word of God to be "dangerous" and frightening. Some people see "signs of the times" in every event that occurs, but often they fail to see the cautionary words Jesus spoke in Matthew 24:4-8:

And Jesus answered and said to them: "Take heed that no one deceives you. For many will come in My name, saying, 'I am the Christ,' and will deceive many. And you will hear of wars and rumors of wars. See that you are not troubled; for all these things must come to pass, but the end is not yet. For nation will rise against nation, and kingdom against kingdom. And there will be famines, pestilences, and earthquakes in various places. All these are the beginning of sorrows.

Such signs will happen but they are only the beginning of sorrows, or birth pains. The key thing we should be looking to concerning the end times and the coming of the Lord is articulated by Jesus in Matthew 24:14, "And this gospel of the Kingdom will be preached in all the world as a witness to all the nations, and then the end will come." The "sign" we ambassadors should be watching is the preaching of the gospel throughout the whole world, then the end will come! Who will do this? Christ's ambassadors! We believers have been mandated with the Great Commission:

Go therefore and make disciples of all the nations, baptizing them in the name of the Father and of the Son and of the Holy Spirit, teaching them to observe all things that I have commanded you; and lo, I am with you always, even to the end of the age. (Matt. 28.19-20).

Jesus will return and the age will end when our mandate is fulfilled. Let's not spend our time focusing on the hour of His return, let's focus our efforts on fulfilling the real sign which will usher in His return. Then the time will come when the King of our Kingdom will recall His ambassadors to Himself! Amen!

7 CONCLUSION

I'm convinced the average Spirit-filled Christian doesn't grasp the concept of living victoriously, nor do they understand the significance of the baptism with the Holy Spirit which empowers them to do so. If we truly did, we would take advantage of this much more than we do. To adequately grasp this requires a renewing of the mind. Such that we no longer live as we used to live, thinking first-birth, but begin to live as new creatures having been born again. As an example of what I'm saying, imagine you were born again at twenty-five years of age. For twenty-five years you thought first-birth. If your body had a pain, your brain gave an answer; "Go to the doctor, or to the medicine cabinet." If you had a financial deficit, your brain had an answer; "Get a loan, or use the credit card." The challenge before the believer now is to be renewed in the spirit of the mind and begin to think "second-birth"! If we have a problem in the natural realm, our first thought should not be a solution in the natural, but to look to the spiritual realm to receive the provision purchased for us by Jesus; to use our faith to receive from God enabling us to rise above and be victorious! Paul the Apostle wrote of this in his Epistle to the Ephesians:

But you have not so learned Christ, if indeed you have heard Him and have been taught by Him, as the truth is in Jesus: that you put off, concerning your former conduct, the old man which grows corrupt according to the deceitful lusts, and be renewed in the spirit of your mind, and that you put on the new man which was created according to God, in true righteousness and holiness. (Eph. 4.20-24).

We are instructed to put on the new man, which after God is created in true righteousness and holiness. In other words, stop identifying with the past and get a new identity! There are two major, serious, identity problems in our modern culture; 1) identity theft and 2) identity crisis. Identity theft is when someone steals another's identity, then pretends to be that person by assuming their identity to gain access to their resources, assets or credit by using their name. Identity crisis, which is actually more serious, is simply defined as someone not knowing who they are. The unresolved crisis actually leaves an individual struggling to find themselves.

Many Christians don't understand who they are in Christ. Often Christians struggle to deal with the past failures or mistakes in their lives. They fail to properly understand when we are born again we become a new creature in Christ according to 2 Corinthians 5:17, "Therefore, if anyone is in Christ, he is a new creation; old things have passed away; behold, all things have become new." We get a new identity! Often Christians think their past is larger than their future, and that's just not so! When we don't know who we are in Christ, it enables Satan to steal our identity, to rob us of the great riches we have in Christ! We are who God says we are. On the cross Jesus purchased and provided things for us. For sickness, He's given us health; for poverty, He's given us wealth. We become citizens of heaven, the righteousness of God in Christ. We're seated together with Christ at God's right hand victorious and more than conquerors. We are at peace with God and complete in Him! Amen!

The true gospel is not clearly understood these days by most people, including many Christians. Much of what is preached and taught today isn't really the true gospel at all! The basic definition of the word "gospel" is, to preach or proclaim good news. It's not proclaiming bad news to people about their situation; rather it is to preach good news. If all a particular speaker has to say is the lost are without hope and doomed to receive judgment of God and eternity in Hell, that isn't good news! That is not a true proclamation of the gospel! There may be truth in some of the things which are said, but simply because one speaks forth some truths does not necessarily mean the gospel has been presented. The good news is, in spite of who you are and what you have done God loves you anyway! The grace of God has extended everything God is to you free of charge! Through Jesus Christ, God has made a way for everyone to be reconciled to Him. It's not based upon your performance and all you have to do is receive it by faith. Now that's good news!

Romans 1:16 contains a tremendous truth for us all to understand, "For I am not ashamed of the gospel of Christ, for it is the power of God to salvation for everyone who believes, for the Jew first and also for the Greek." This verse clearly teaches the gospel is the power which accomplishes salvation in the life of a believer. Unfortunately, the word "salvation" doesn't carry all the meaning and significance in the English language that it does in the original Greek language. When we think about salvation we tend to connect it to eternal life and forgiveness of our sins. It is true that our salvation includes these benefits but it also includes much more. The word "salvation" actually includes everything the Lord Jesus Christ purchased for us by His death and resurrection; healing, deliverance, prosperity, and soundness – everything God desires for you! The power which accomplishes this for us is the gospel of Christ. There are many people who are born again and have a genuine relationship with God who do not have the power in them to produce the things they need. There are lots of people who believe God is the answer, but fail to experience answers to the problems in their lives. There are believers who experience no more victory than those who do not believe. There are people who believe in healing, but not healed, who believe in prosperity but not prosperous, who believe in deliverance but remain under oppression. Why is this so? I believe it is because of the way many have been taught to believe the gospel. Many people live below their rights and privileges in Christ because of a failure to believe or correctly understand the gospel. Unfortunately, over the years, in an attempt to explain the Church's lack of power and inability to experience answers to problems, doctrines of men have surfaced. Too often the Church has been passive and inactive, relinquishing all responsibility, thinking whatever will be, will be and everything which happens is the will of God. That is bad doctrine! Jesus took hold of the will of God and prayed and ministered with an active faith to accomplish the will of God in the earth! We in the Church must do the same. Romans 1:16 teaches us God has made a way for every Christian to experience victory in their lives. We must be willing to acknowledge if we are failing to experience answers, somewhere or some way we do not fully believe or understand the gospel. Because the power is in the gospel to accomplish salvation! If Romans 1:16 is true and it is, then it cannot be God who is withholding His power and blessings from us! If necessary we must "Repent, and believe in the gospel." (Mk. 1.15). Some need to change the way they have been thinking about the gospel, and believe every good and perfect gift from God is ours! (Jas. 1.17). Our good God has truly provided a complete and perfect salvation for us.

Accomplish Your Dream

An important part of living victoriously is fulfilling our God-given destiny. God has created each of us with purpose. We have to discover what it is and then set ourselves on a course to complete it. In order to complete God's plan for our lives it will be necessary for us to *conceive* the vision, *believe* the vision and then *achieve* the vision.

Conceive

There are people who desire to be mightily used of God. On the way toward "mighty" there is a process which begins with conception. Saul of Tarsus had an experience with the Lord which propelled him toward later becoming the Apostle Paul. In Acts 9:4-6 we read:

> Then he fell to the ground, and heard a voice saying to him, "Saul, Saul, why are you persecuting Me?" And he said, "Who are You, Lord?" Then the Lord said, "I am Jesus, whom you are persecuting. It is hard for you to kick against the goads." So he, trembling and astonished, said, "Lord, what do You want me to do?" Then the Lord said to him, "Arise and go into the city, and you will be told what you must do."

Saul was on the road to Damascus, authorized by the religious leaders, for the purpose of further persecuting the Church. Jesus confronted him on the road and said to him, "Why are you persecuting Me?" Saul wasn't persecuting Jesus personally; he was persecuting the Church, but Jesus took it very personally! Saul of Tarsus was a religious terrorist attempting to destroy the Church of Jesus Christ and may have done a good job of completing the task if Jesus had not intervened! Saul's response to Jesus' question was, "Who are You Lord?" It's interesting that he referred to Him as Lord. Can you imagine the sense of shame and guilt he must have felt when he realized the recipient of his blasphemous acts was Jesus the Lord? Jesus told him, "It is hard for you to kick against the goads." A goad was a pointed instrument used to prod animals. The animals would kick at the goad to resist it. Apparently Saul had been resisting the Lord's conviction for some time. Saul then responded saying, "Lord, what do you want me to do?" A very important question which we all need an answer to.

As a result of the experience he was unable to see for a period of three days. (Acts 9.8-9). We're told he was led by the hand to Damascus. In the meantime, God was dealing with a man by the name of Ananias, instructing him to go and minister to this Saul of Tarsus. (Acts 9.10-14). We're told the Lord said to Ananias, "…he is a chosen vessel of Mine to bear My name before Gentiles, kings, and the children of Israel." (Acts 9.15). When God reveals His purpose to you it is important that you respond in faith to conceive it in your heart! You have a part to play in it. You must be a participant in bringing its fulfillment. God's will is not automatic. Your part is to be willing and cooperate by faith! You have to capture the vision for your life. What does it mean to capture the vision for your life? Ted Engstrom, the former president of World Vision, told a story which went something like this:

> A little girl was on a cruise ship, and she and her father were standing on the deck. It was a beautiful clear day, and the air was crisp and fresh. The little girl, standing on tiptoe, said to her father, "I can't see anything." The father picked her up and put her on his shoulders, so that she was higher than everyone else on the deck and was able to see everything around her. "Daddy!" she exclaimed. "I can see farther than my eyes can look!" (Munroe, "Principles and Power…" 16-17).

Vision is the ability to see farther than your eyes can look. To see not just what is, but also what can be. And then begin to move in that direction to make it a reality. Most people tend to focus only on what their physical eyes can see, which limits what God can do through them. Some believe their past experiences such as lack of education, social or spiritual failures, or other mistakes from the past disqualify them. Sometimes we think our past is larger than our future! Paul the Apostle's past as Saul of Tarsus the terrorist didn't disqualify him, and our past doesn't disqualify us either. No, your past doesn't change God's purpose for you!

Believe

It's easy to get excited about a vision, but it is harder to be faithful to it. Faithfulness to the vision is one of the marks of its legitimacy. In Acts twenty-six, Paul was on trial before King Agrippa. As he told the King about the purpose he received from Jesus on the road to Damascus, he made a statement which is very important concerning people with vision:

> So I said, 'Who are You, Lord?' And He said, 'I am Jesus, whom you are persecuting. But rise and stand on your feet; for I have appeared to you for this purpose, to make you a minister and a witness both of the things which you have seen and of the things which I will yet reveal to you. I will deliver you from the Jewish people, as well as from the Gentiles, to whom I now send you, to open their eyes, in order to turn them from darkness to light, and from the power of Satan to God, that they may receive forgiveness of sins and an inheritance among those who are sanctified by faith in Me.' (Acts 26.15-18).

After recounting his experience, he said in verse nineteen, "Therefore, King Agrippa, I was not disobedient to the heavenly vision." Paul knew what his purpose was in life, and it kept him going through all his struggles. You must believe in and value your heavenly vision. I wonder how many of God's people have given up too soon for various reasons.

How many have quit, thinking, "It is taking too long"? Sometimes we wonder when the dream will come to pass. How many give up on accomplishing their vision because "It is too hard" wondering how long to endure? You will have to learn to stand when trouble and hardships come. If you are going to be what you see in your mind, you will have to believe what you have in your heart!

Achieve

At the end of Paul's third missionary journey he was leaving Asia Minor, and before he left he called together the elders from Ephesus to exhort them one more time and to say goodbye. Knowing persecutions awaited him he made the comment in Acts 20:24:

> But none of these things move me; nor do I count my life dear to myself, so that I may finish my race with joy, and the ministry which I received from the Lord Jesus, to testify to the gospel of the grace of God.

With the knowledge of persecutions awaiting he said, "none of these things move me; nor do I count my life dear to myself." One hindrance to finishing the race with joy is counting your life too dear to yourself. Don't misunderstand my comment. I believe God will give us a good life, and we should have lives we love but we should not love life more than we love Jesus or the desire to finish our race. Difficulties in life shouldn't derail us. Starting the race isn't enough, we should be able to finish our race with joy! 1 Thessalonians 5:16-18 tells us to, "Rejoice always, pray without ceasing, in everything give thanks; for this is the will of God in Christ Jesus for you." I strongly believe rejoicing and thankfulness are super important ingredients to have which enable us to finish our race with joy and to be able to achieve our God-given dream. Joyful rejoicing and thankfulness will repel discouragement. The New Testament refers to our God-given lives as a race in other places. Hebrews 12:1 exhorts, "Therefore we also, since we are surrounded by so great a cloud of witnesses, let us lay aside every weight, and the sin which so easily ensnares us, and let us run with endurance the race that is set before us…" and also in 1 Corinthians 9:24, "Do you not know that those who run in a race all run, but one receives the prize? Run in such a way that you may obtain it." The Scripture likens our lives to a race, I particularly like to think of it in terms of a relay race. Because none of us are in this alone. Our individual lives are only a part of the big picture. We are all working together as one body accomplishing the will of God in the earth.

Run Your Race

I have never been a good runner. In high school my sports were primarily football and track. I was a lineman on offense and defense in football. And I was a member of the track team but not as a runner. I threw shot put and discus. I remember one particular time very well. We were preparing one week for the weekend Invitational Track Meet to be held in Buena Vista, Colorado. Myself and three other shot put throwers were practicing together at the shot put ring on a Monday afternoon preparing for Saturday's track meet. I noticed the team's head coach, Bill Meigs, was walking across the infield in our direction. Coach Meigs was an older gentleman who had been a member of the Florence High School faculty for many years. He taught the Automobile Mechanics classes in the vocational department of our school. I knew him from those classes as well. He was a good man; I liked him. He enjoyed coaching the boys track team at our school which he had done for many years. I noticed that afternoon he was still headed in our direction. Walking at a quick pace, he arrived at our practice ring and said, "You boys come with me." He led us out onto the track and explained to us he wanted to enter us as his second team in the mile relay race in Saturday's track meet! Apparently he had been thinking about it and was aware the competition would not be so great for the mile relay. He wanted to enter a second team in the race which could hopefully win additional team points if we could place. He began to work with us, coaching us each day to prepare us for the race. He began with the passing of the baton. He explained to us that there is a critical moment in every relay race which can determine the outcome. Which is the passing of the baton. If the baton is dropped, basically it means, game over. So we practiced every day that week in preparation for the race.

Race day came. We were signed up as one of the teams from our school for the mile relay. That year our track team had a really good mile relay team made up of fast and capable runners. In fact, they were state championship contenders. Our time to race came. We were in the same heat as our first mile relay team. I was to run the third leg of the race. When the gun sounded, off they went. After the first lap our primary mile relay team was well into the lead with no serious competition. The race was now for second place. My friend, Ron Gasser, was running our second leg. He was a large, overweight teenage shot put thrower no one would have thought of as a runner. Gasser took the baton with our team in second place. I then took my place on the track and waited for him to get to me. When the group rounded the second curve of the track, big Gasser was still in second place! He had managed to hold his position. He handed the baton off to me successfully and I began to run. Soon I could hear the steps and breathing of the runner behind me. In those days the tracks were constructed of cinder. You could hear the crunch under your feet each step you took. I could hear the crunch and heavy breathing of the person behind me who seemed to be catching me! I was afraid I was losing my lead! I could hear the breathing…whew, whew, whew and the crunch, crunch, crunch as we rounded the first curve. I wanted to turn and look behind me so bad! But in my mind I could hear Coach Meigs' words, "Just run your race. Don't worry about what others are doing." It's a great mistake for a runner to take his eyes off of the track and attempt to look around. I chose to try to not think about the runner behind me and focus on my race. I spoke to myself in my mind, "Just pace yourself...run your race...do what you're supposed to do." By the time I made my way down the back stretch I realized I was no longer hearing the runner behind me. He had burned himself out too early; I was actually widening the lead! I passed the baton, the last runner on our team held on. The shot put throwers won second place!

There are tremendous spiritual lessons to be learned from racing. One has to keep their eyes on the prize and not look back. This is actually brought out in Hebrews 12:2, which follows the exhortation to "run with endurance the race that is set before us." (verse one), "looking unto Jesus, the author and finisher of our faith, who for the joy that was set before Him endured the cross, despising the shame, and has sat down at the right hand of the throne of God."

Jesus is one of the great cloud of witnesses today cheering us on. He's been to the cross for us. He's purchased our freedom and the forgiveness of our sins. He is offering the great riches of God's grace to us. He's given us access to the empowering presence of the Holy Spirit so we can be victorious. Now it is necessary for us to run our race with endurance knowing we have truly been equipped and born again to win!

APPENDIX A: Prayer for Salvation

The most important choice you will make in your life is to receive or reject Jesus. If you have never accepted Jesus as your personal Savior, I encourage you to do it today. If you cannot remember a time when you prayed to confess Jesus as Lord of your life, you are gambling with your life. Jesus said, "Do not marvel that I said to you, you must be born again." (John 3:7).

The way to be born again is to pray a simple prayer based upon Romans 10:9-10

> ...that if you confess with your mouth the Lord Jesus and believe in your heart that God has raised Him from the dead, you will be saved. For with the heart one believes unto righteousness, and with the mouth confession is made unto salvation.

If you truly believe in Jesus and believe in your heart that God sent Him to die for your sins, and that God raised Him from the dead for your justification, the only thing left for you to do is make the choice to act on what you believe to confess Jesus as Lord. You can do it by praying the following prayer sincerely from your heart:

Heavenly Father, I believe You sent Jesus to die for my sins. I believe You raised Him from the dead. And I choose Jesus today. I confess that Jesus is my Lord. I ask You to forgive me of my sins. I now turn away from my past and I turn to You, to live for You for the rest of my life. Thank You for loving me, for forgiving me, and for saving me. In Jesus' name I pray. Amen.

APPENDIX B: Prayer to Receive the Baptism with the Holy Spirit

As I have stated in chapter four, the Promise of the Father is available to every believer. If you have made Jesus your personal Lord and Savior the next step for you is to go ahead and receive the Baptism with the Holy Spirit. The greatest thing I have ever received from the Lord, next to the forgiveness of my sins and salvation is when I was filled with the Holy Spirit.

If you have understood what I have explained in chapter four, I encourage you to pray the following prayer in faith believing to receive the Baptism with the Holy Spirit. Expect God to fill you and expect Him to give you an utterance of other tongues in your spirit. Then cooperate with Him by faith using your mouth, voice, and tongue to articulate the utterance by faith. Remember, the Holy Spirit does not speak in tongues. He gives the utterance, and you will speak it forth. Will you do it? If you will, then you will. If you won't, you won't. You have to be willing to cooperate and receive it by faith. God will do His part; He's not the variable. Pray the following prayer in faith believing:

Heavenly Father, I come to You to receive the gift of the Promise of the Father. I'm asking You to baptize me with Your Spirit right now with the evidence of speaking in other tongues. I thank You that You hear me and You have filled me with Your Spirit. I receive it now. In Jesus' name I pray. Amen.

Some syllables from a language you have never learned will rise up from your spirit. As you speak them out loud by faith you are releasing God's power from within. If you believed in your heart that you received from Him, God's Word promises you did. Now exercise it regularly. This isn't simply a one-time experience! May God bless you richly!

Michael R. McComb

BIBLIOGRAPHY

Blackhouse, Robert. *The Kregel Pictorial Guide to the Temple*. Grand Rapids: Kregel Publications, 1996. Print.

Edersheim, Alfred. *Sketches of Jewish Social Life*. Updated ed. Peabody: Hendrickson, 1994. Print.

Hagin, Kenneth E. *The Spirit Within & The Spirit Upon*. Tulsa: Rhema Bible Church, 2003. Print.

---. *Tongues Beyond the Upper Room*. Tulsa: Rhema Bible Church, 2007. Print.

Hayford, Jack W. *The Hayford Bible Handbook*. Nashville: Thomas Nelson, 1995. Print.

---. *Spirit Filled Life Bible*. Nashville: Thomas Nelson, 1991. Print. Kingdom Dynamics: The Gospel of the Kingdom

Menzies, William W., and Stanley M. Horton. *Bible Doctrines: A Pentecostal Perspective*. Springfield: Logion, 1996. Print.

Munroe, Myles. *The Principles and Power of Vision: Keys to Achieving Personal and Corporate Destiny*. New Kensington: Whitaker House, 2003. Print.

---. *Rediscovering the Kingdom*. Expanded ed. Shippensburg: Destiny Image, 2010. Print.

Renner, Rick. *A Light in Darkness: Seven Messages to the Seven Churches*. Vol. 1. Tulsa: Teach All Nations, 2010. Print.

Strong, James. *Strong's Exhaustive Concordance*. Compact ed. Grand Rapids: Baker Book House, 1982. Print.

Voight, Robert G. *The Complete Perfect Salvation in Christ Jesus*. Tulsa:

Oral Roberts U, 1988. Print.

Weymouth, Richard Francis. *The New Testament in Modern Speech*. Ft. Worth: Kenneth Copeland Publications, 1996. Print.

Wommack, Andrew. *Life for Today: Study Bible and Commentary*. The I & II Corinthians ed. United States of America: Andrew Wommack Ministries, 1996. Print.

---. *Life for Today: Study Bible and Commentary*. The Acts of the Apostles ed. United States of America: Andrew Wommack Ministries, 1994. Print.

---. *Life for Today: Study Bible and Commentary*. The Galatians, Ephesians, Philippians and Colossians ed. United States of America: Andrew Wommack Ministries, 1998. Print.

---. *Life for Today: Study Bible and Commentary*. The Gospels ed. United States of America: Andrew Wommack Ministries, 1992. Print.

Yandian, Bob. *Fellowshipping with God: Why We Speak in Tongues*. Tulsa: Bob Yandian Ministries, 1998. Print.

---. *Understanding the End Times*. Tulsa: Bob Yandian Ministries, 2001. Print.

Unless otherwise indicated, all scriptural quotations are from the *New King James Version* of the Bible.

ABOUT THE AUTHOR

For the past 25 years Michael McComb has served in pastoral ministry overseeing three different churches during that time span. He currently pastors Church on the Inside which is the name he has chosen for the congregation behind the walls of the Kyle Correctional Center in Kyle, Texas. He has served as the Chaplain at that facility since July 1999.

He is a graduate of Christ for the Nations Institute in Dallas, Texas as well as Charis Bible College in Woodland Park, Colorado. In addition, he has earned his Bachelor and Master's degrees and a Doctor of Ministry in Theology from Life Christian University in Tampa, Florida.

His passion is to advance God's Kingdom by teaching the Bible with a strong emphasis on Grace and Faith. In addition to his pastoral responsibilities as a Chaplain he has served as Director of Life Christian Bible Institute in Austin/Lockhart, Texas since September 2006.

To contact the author, e-mail:

mikemccombministries@gmail.com

58783186R00105

Made in the USA
Charleston, SC
19 July 2016